The New
Commodity
Trading Guide

The New Commodity Trading Guide

Breakthrough Strategies for Capturing Market Profits

GEORGE KLEINMAN

Vice President, Publisher: Tim Moore
Associate Publisher and Director of Marketing: Amy Neidlinger
Executive Editor: Jim Boyd
Editorial Assistant: Myesha Graham
Operations Manager: Gina Kanouse
Digital Marketing Manager: Julie Phifer
Publicity Manager: Laura Czaja
Assistant Marketing Manager: Megan Colvin
Cover Designer: Chuti Prasertsith
Managing Editor: Kristy Hart
Project Editor: Betsy Harris
Copy Editor: Krista Hansing Editorial Services, Inc.
Proofreader: San Dee Phillips
Senior Indexer: Cheryl Lenser
Senior Compositor: Gloria Schurick
Manufacturing Buyer: Dan Uhrig

This book is sold with the understanding that neither the author nor the publisher is engaged in rendering financial, investment, legal, accounting, or other professional services or advice by publishing this book. Each individual situation is unique. Thus, if legal or financial advice or other expert assistance is required in a specific situation, the services of a competent professional should be sought to ensure that the situation has been evaluated carefully and appropriately. The author and the publisher disclaim any liability, loss, or risk resulting directly or indirectly, from the use or application of any of the contents of this book.

Before you trade with real money, familiarize yourself with the risks.

Important Risk Disclosures: Commodity futures trading is speculative, involves substantial risks, and you should invest only risk capital.

You can lose a substantial amount or all your investment, and therefore you should carefully consider whether such trading is suitable for you in light of your financial condition.

The high degree of leverage that is obtainable in commodity trading can work against you as well as for you—the use of leverage can lead to large losses as well as large gains.

If the market moves against your position, to maintain your position you may on short notice be called upon by your broker to deposit additional margin money. If funds are requested, and you do not provide them within the prescribed time, your position may be liquidated at a loss, and you will be liable for any resulting deficit in your account. Under certain market conditions, you may find it difficult or impossible to liquidate a position. This can occur, for example, when the market makes a "limit move." The placement of contingent orders, such as a "stop-loss" or "stop-limit" order, will not necessarily limit your losses to the intended amount.

There is no guarantee that the concepts presented in this book will generate profits or avoid losses.

Past results are not necessarily indicative of future results.

All charts courtesy of CQG, Inc.

CQG, Inc. © 2008 All rights reserved worldwide.

Library of Congress Cataloging-in-Publication Data

Kleinman, George.

  The new commodity trading guide : breakthrough strategies for capturing market profits / George Kleinman.

    p. cm.

  ISBN 0-13-714529-2 (hardback : alk. paper) 1. Commodity futures. 2. Commodity exchanges. 3. Investment analysis. I. Title. II. Title: Commodity trading guide.

  HG6046.K53 2009

  332.64'4—dc22

                                        2008039902

As always, for Sherri

Contents

Acknowledgments

Thanks to my editors at Pearson—Jim Boyd, Betsy Harris, and Krista Hansing—for making my thoughts flow better. Thanks to the people at CQG for their premier analytical and trading software who made possible the many charts without which this book would not have been possible. Thanks to my best clients—you know who you are. Mary Cashman, who pens *Global Market Intelligence*, has helped me shape my market views, and Yiannis Mostrous from KCI has always been totally supportive. Sincere thanks to Nancy Torok for assisting me daily and by necessity putting up with me, and also my family, who has no choice but to put up with me: Sherri, Kevin, Craig, and Hayley, who recently gave us our first granddaughter, Leah.

About the Author

George Kleinman is the president of the successful futures advisory, brokerage, and trading firm Commodity Resource Corp. George founded CRC in 1983 from the "floor" of the Minneapolis Grain Exchange to offer a more personalized level of service to commodity traders. He entered the business with Merrill Lynch Commodities (1978–1983). At Merrill he attained the honor of Golden Circle—one of Merrill's top ten commodity brokers internationally. He is a graduate of The Ohio State University and also has an MBA from Hofstra University. George was a member of various commodity exchanges for more than 25 years and is the author of three previous books on commodities and futures trading. He is executive editor of the commodity trading advisory service *Futures Market Forecaster*. In 1995, George relocated to northern Nevada and today trades from his office overlooking beautiful Lake Tahoe.

Going the Way of the Dodo

"Men, it has been well said, think in herds; it will be seen that they go mad in herds, while they only recover their senses slowly, and one by one."
—Charles Mackay, 1841, *Memoirs of Extraordinary Popular Delusions and the Madness of Crowds*

The dodo, a flightless bird, has been extinct since the 17th century.

According to Wikipedia, the verb phrase to "go the way of the dodo" means to become obsolete, to fall out of common usage, or to become a thing of the past. The dodo is considered the poster child for an extinct species because its demise was directly attributable to human activity. (They were good to eat and easy to catch.)

Have you ever wondered whether the last dodo bird was aware of being the very last one?

On the first trading day of 2008, the price of crude oil easily exceeded $99 per barrel, due to a Nigerian rebel attack on oil-producing facilities. The rumor circulating trading desks globally was that this would be *the* day—the first day in history that oil prices would trade at that psychological stratospheric barrier of $100 per barrel.

I was watching the oil market that day and saw it approach $100, but it never quite reached it. The market traded at a new all-time high of approximately $99.00 but then ran out of steam and rolled over. Oil prices continued trading lower just as I received a "Breaking News" e-mail from *Marketwatch* that read: "Oil trades at $100 for the first time ever." I turned to my assistant and asked her what she showed as the high crude oil price. "It's $99.81," Nancy told me. "Last print, $99.50." So I looked at the other delivery months, but they were all trading at a discount—not even close to $100. I thought to myself, they just got it wrong this time.

That night, I was watching the evening news on NBC and the anchor reported: "Oil in New York traded today, for the first time ever, at $100 per barrel." "How could they all get this so wrong?" I thought. Then it dawned on me. Like most traders, I was watching the electronic oil market where more than 99% of all trades take place. I didn't think to check the pit market that hardly anyone traded on or looked at anymore. Sure enough, "the pit" had recorded a different high than "the screen"—exactly $100 per barrel. The wire services had picked up on this feat and reported it as headline news around the world. Of course, this raised the question, why would anyone pay more than the market when they could have easily bought at the screen price? The pit trade is fast disappearing because it's slower than electronic trading. Was this merely an aberration?

The next day, the full story came out. On January 2, 2008, 747,748 one-thousand-barrel contracts changed hands, with 99% of them trading on the screen and just one of those contracts trading at the price of $100. This lone contract changed hands (as we had already discovered) in the pit. I really wouldn't call this a "legitimate" trade, even though an exchange spokesman called it just that in a press release the following day. The man behind this record-high price was an anonymous professional pit trader. Did he make a mistake?

No, he knew exactly what he was doing. This guy was willing to lose $300 for bragging rights. The BBC subsequently termed this a "vanity trade." He absolutely overpaid for the right to tell his grandkids, "I was the first person in history to buy $100 oil."

This "achievement" will no doubt turn out to be one of the last hurrahs of the pit trader. Electronic trading is faster, cheaper, more efficient, and, in certain ways, more honest than having market makers take the other side of a trade. These are the reasons why the pit trader is fast "going the way of the dodo," and as with that tasty flightless bird, the pit trader's demise is directly attributable to human activity.

It's Different This Time?

As you read *The New Commodity Trading Guide,* be aware that "New" will always be in the title whenever you read this. So at what point does this book become similar to the pit trader—obsolete and no longer "new"?

The book presents commodity trading in a new light because I believe the commodity markets perform differently today than any time before. During most of my career, which spans more than 30 years, futures trading was viewed as a casino. Now many financial planners treat commodities as an asset class, and they allocate a portion of their portfolios to commodities alongside traditional stocks and bonds. Then consider the electronic factor that has dramatically changed the way the markets behave. Add in increased demand from the emerging economies, the hedge funds and the index funds, and you've planted the seeds for change. Because the commodity markets act differently now, new techniques are required for trading success. Still, it's important to remember that these four words—"it's different this time"—have collectively resulted in more lost money for more traders than any others.

A few years after the 1929 stock market crash, the great trader and philanthropist Bernard Baruch wrote a foreword to a reprint of Charles Mackay's classic *Extraordinary Popular Delusions and the Madness of Crowds.* Originally published in 1841, Mackay's book chronicled various investment manias from the 1500s through the 1800s. From the tulip craze to the Mississippi and South Sea Bubbles, the basic underlying premise was that manias (economic and otherwise) are a condition of the human species. They will come and go over time but never disappear. My reprinted edition of *Popular Delusions* was published in October 1932, right in the thick of the Great Depression. In this quote from the foreword, Baruch refers to that most recent mania he termed the "1929 market madness in America": "I have often thought that if, in the lamentable era of the 'New Economics,' culminating in 1929, even in the presence of dizzily spiraling prices, we had all continuously repeated, 'two and two still make four,' much of the evil might have been averted." Those very words could be used today; just substitute the dates.

The 1929 panic and eventual recovery from the Great Depression that followed were not firsts for America. Crashes and market panics occurred in 1837, 1857, 1861, 1873, 1893, 1901, and one could make a case for 2008 as well. The 1857 panic was preceded by the California gold rush. The 1873 panic was preceded by a speculatively induced bubble in railroad stocks. The panic of 2008 was preceded by a speculative boom in housing prices that created the subprime debacle. Still, more has been written about the 1929 crash than any other crash in history because more people in the newly minted middle and upper classes were affected, and also because few people saw it coming. People held a widespread belief at that time in the "new economics"¹ A period of permanent prosperity had arrived. Certainly, the 1920s was an unprecedented period of prosperity, with new wealth created from the automobile industry and the accompanying boom in road building and travel. A plethora of new technologies and new household electronic appliances, such as the radio, were born. To top it all off, the 1920s saw the creation and widespread use of installment credit products. Perhaps this was one of the main unsung underlying causes of the crash. Looking at modern history, we can point to the dotcom mania of the late 1990s. In recent years, examples include the condo mania in Florida and Las Vegas and the subprime housing crisis in California and many other places. Obscure manias also pop up nearly every year but fail to reach the mainstream media because they affect only a few of those directly involved. (I chronicle one of these, with the accompanying valuable lessons, in Chapter 2, "Capturing a 5,000% Return," a recent commodity bubble that ended with the inevitable burst.)

One shared trait of all manias is that the majority of players never see the collapse coming. If you read the financial press from 1929 to 1931, all during the period the market was falling, respected analysts continually considered it a correction that would soon be over. When stocks finally did hit bottom in 1933, more than 80% of all value had been lost. Will this be how the current commodity boom ends? Will today's commodity bubble burst? The answer to this question is, yes, it certainly will end badly because the history of mankind is that all economic bubbles eventually burst. The only question is, when? It will take place after any bull market move in a particular commodity market morphs into a mania. This will be the time when the general public is totally immersed in the story of the day. It's never "different this time": It always ends the same way—badly for the general public. However, as this is being written, I question the premise that, in a macro sense, this commodity bull run is anything close to a mania or a bubble. It's more similar to a balloon, inflating and deflating but overall somewhere at the half inflation point. Before the 1929 stock market crash, shares in shell companies were being manufactured without economic justification, and only because people would buy them. In contrast, commodities have intrinsic value and are being consumed by those who buy them.

So how will we know the final top is in for commodities as an asset class?

When analyzing any market move for a top, ask yourself whether the market you're looking at is currently spiraling. Does it look similar to a flagpole growing up to the sky (which the laws of physics tell us cannot last indefinitely), or has it recently been cleansed and purged via a healthy correction? In the middle of a move, some of the air (the buying) that was pumped in flows out before new air is pumped in. One of my goals for this book is to teach you how to recognize the early signs of a new bull run, and also how to recognize the end of the run.

One type of top is the blow-off top, a formation that occurs at the end a sustained bull market run. How can you tell if a market is in a blow-off top? Close to the end of the move, during the top formation, the market surges higher, with only shallow corrections. Compared to the norm, volumes are huge. Technical indicators such as the RSI (an oscillator) run up to extremely high (overbought) readings, but although these readings appear to be in unsustainable territory, the market continues moving higher than anyone believed possible. Then you'll hear outlandish price predictions in the mainstream media, and talk of shortages will be rampant. The talk will be that the world is going to run out of this or that. In many cases, the last 48 hours of a major move can be the most feverish—and the most lucrative for the bulls. This final surge that forms the actual blow-off is the most painful for the bears. Their capitulation (short covering) creates the final high prices. Nobody I know of is able to pick the exact top in a situation such as this. However, in markets that show these signs, if you have been fortunate enough to be on for some of the ride, it's time to be vigilant because the end is near. The top price will come when nobody is looking and generally when the news is as bullish as it can get.

Most people will see the first break from the top price as a normal correction, just a temporary break within a bull that is nowhere close to being over yet. The market might have a secondary rally after the first break, but then it will be unable to register new highs. Without most of the players realizing it's happening, the air will be let out of the bubble. Then one day it will whoosh. Bullish news might continue during much of the move back down. At some point, the bull turns into a bear, the decline accelerates, and ultimately there's *blood in the streets*. This is the time when the news will turn very bearish, there will be a multiyear surplus of this or that, and it will appear that the bear has settled in for the long pull. In reality, as only the smart money will see during blood in the streets, the bear is losing the game and will soon be replaced by a young bull.

As this is being written, the macro forces of a continuing global commodity bull trend appear to remain in force. The balloon is inflating, not deflating. Sure, there have been, and will continue to be, plenty of healthy corrections along the way, but consider these merely temporary tops.

Let's briefly discuss the fundamentals that lead me to believe this current commodity bull will be running for quite some time yet. We know explosive demand growth exists in the developing world, with no easy way to turn this train around. More than a billion consumers are moving up to a higher level of consumption, demanding the comforts the West has enjoyed since the third Industrial Revolution that began in the early 1900s. For many decades, one billion of Earth's human inhabitants have consumed two-thirds of Earth's developed resources. The other six billion got by on the remaining third. Now, led by China and India, the developing world is eating better and living better, and this requires massive commodity consumption. These people are transitioning from being mainly producers to a combination of producers and consumers. From a macro sense, this places upward pressure on commodity prices.

The magnitude of this unprecedented demand shock is difficult to comprehend, as these people drive more cars and consume more protein and electric power. Heating, lighting, air conditioning, and appliances require power plants. New buildings, roads, ships, ports, trains, trucks, and buses—the list goes on. Energy needs, food requirements, textiles, copper to build new electrical grids, corn and soybean meal to feed growing populations of pigs, chicken, and cattle. Soybeans, cotton, rice, sugar, and corn for food and fuel, with more fertilizer needed to grow these crops.

The global population is growing at 80 million people annually. This is the equivalent of adding one Mexico to the world every year. The areas of the world with the greatest population percentage increases are moving toward the consumption patterns of the developed world. And while all this is taking place, the developed world continues to consume. And it's not just India and China that are players in this industrial revolution. Other rapidly emerging Asian nations, Eastern Europeans, Russians, and South Americans (with Brazil in the forefront) are all creating massive new consumer middle classes. But let's concentrate on China for a few paragraphs.

As we go to press, the average American is using approximately 25 barrels' worth of oil annually. To put this number in perspective, at the conclusion of World War II when the Japanese economy was in ruins, the Japanese consumed the equivalent of one barrel per capita annually. Now that Japan has become a modern industrialized power, the average Japanese person consumes approximately 17 barrels of oil annually. A decade ago, the average Chinese person consumed about one barrel annually, and now this number is rapidly approaching two. What happens when this number doubles again and then quadruples? On a daily basis, the world is using all the oil it can produce. For example, we have about 900 cars for every 1,000 people in the United States. By comparison (and this number is constantly growing and will be outdated by the time you read it), only 45 people per 1,000 own cars in China. If vehicle ownership there doubles to 90, how will this affect the demand for aluminum and rubber in auto manufacturing? China recently surpassed the United States as the world's largest copper consumer. And what about oil? As we know, a large percentage of global oil supplies are produced in volatile places. China is an oil importer, and as its oil consumption grows, what happens every time a disruption occurs due to an outage, pipeline problem, hurricane, war, or some political event in a producing country? Chinese per-capita income has risen from less than $500 in 1990 to $3,000 in 2008, and Indian per-capita income has risen from less than $500 in 1990 to more than $1,000 in 2008. This stimulates energy demand, not to mention demand for more and better food.

North American farmers have experienced great growing weather for most of the past 100 years. This benefit, combined with improvements in agriculture, has resulted in abundant crops. You have to go back 800 years to find a period of such favorable weather for such a long time. Yet as 2008 has shown, we know what can happen to the price of wheat, for example, if a few crop failures occur around the world—prices can easily triple. Considering how good weather has generally been during the past two decades; food stocks in corn, wheat, soybeans, and rice seem to remain dangerously low year after year. With another Mexico being added to the world's population each year, the demand side of the equation will not solve this problem. With global warming an impending dilemma for crops, can the world continue to rely on the supply side growing? When the world again experiences a year of bad weather (whether too much rain or too little, temperatures too hot or too cold), food prices are set to surge again.

Fundamentals are important because they set the tone for commodity price moves. However, increasingly in this new electronic age, fundamental analyses will not help you in your trading. The fundamentals for many of the markets we trade are complex and often conflicting. I've designed this book to help the individual trader. With that in mind, realize that it's virtually impossible for an individual to sort through the thousands of statistics that comprise the European economy to accurately determine the direction the Euro will be moving today. Many traders have wondered why something like this happens: On the day it was announced that the supplies of crude oil went down an extremely bullish five million barrels in the weekly report (and the traders were looking for an increase), how could the market close lower? Apparently, some hidden evil fundamental must have been lurking ("evil" because we were long that day) that caused that crash. As with the European currency, the fundamentals for oil (and all the other commodities, for that matter) are complex. During any particular trading session, assembling all the supply and demand data bits into a trading strategy is impossible. However, you can analyze one dominant fundamental to achieve profitability.

George Soros wrote, "The most important fundamental is credit flow"—or to put this more simply, *money*. *Money flows* move markets, and this is the most important determinant of price action. My premise is that you need to correctly analyze only this one fundamental to be successful: which direction the money is flowing. How do we do this? This book addresses that very question. As we go to press, the time is still ripe to capitalize on the continuing macro bull trend in commodities. However, when it does finally come to an end, the book won't be obsolete. My plan is to also help you capitalize on the bear trend, and I explore techniques and methodologies—for both scenarios.

Our topic is as old as the hills. Commodities are necessary for life and comfort, and will continue to be traded as long as the human race exists. Every economy has experienced long periods of negative growth when commodity prices were depressed (as some are today). Then the bull cycles occur. Today the current global bull commodity cycle is about a decade old. Mini cycles, such as the commodity decade of the 1970s, lasted about ten years. However, long-term charts beginning in the 1700s tell us that major bull cycles in commodities generally range from 18 to 23 years. For example, as humankind entered the twentieth century, the last (the third great) Industrial Revolution lasted nearly 30 years. How long will this one last? I am a good enough student of mass psychology to know that this book will remain popular only as long as commodities are in a bull cycle. The public is not interested in bear cycles. So perhaps one way to determine whether the globe is still experiencing a bull commodity cycle is to ask where you bought (and I do hope you bought) *The New Commodity Trading Guide*? Did you buy it new at full price, or used at a discount? The latter might be an indication that this cycle has run its course.

In my current time frame, as this is being written, America, and by contagion much of the globe, is going through a colossal financial crisis. The major investments banks of Bear Stearns and Lehman Brothers, both in business for more than 100 years, are now both gone. The U.S. government has bailed out Freddie Mac and Fannie Mae and taken over AIG, and there will be additional bailouts and more money printing ahead of us. It's a real financial mess, with countless paper assets plummeting in value. Although liquidity problems can bleed over into commodity values at times, unlike the stock or bond of a failed financial entity, commodity prices will always rebound because they are necessary to sustain and enhance life.

I anticipate that commodities will continue to be hot for years to come because the world has entered a period of tightening commodity supplies with increasing demand. The planet's resources are limited, and commodities can play a role in your asset-allocation decisions. However, if the cycle has run its course, realize that bear cycles can be as profitable as their counterpart, and they can move much faster. Just follow the money flows.

Perhaps as you read this, oil use will have been replaced by some alternative energy source, but the macro trend of accelerating commodity consumption will likely continue unabated. More important, the trend of accelerating power usage will continue, and the new challenge will be avoiding power shortages. No quick solution exists for electricity shortages, and I anticipate that this will become a growing problem as global power demand accelerates. Many of the best trading opportunities lie ahead of us, but be aware of ebb and flow to all of this. There's a time for all things, and one day the bull will lose control and then the bear will take over. As you read this, I have no way of knowing whether the bull or the bear is winning the race you choose to join this week.

Baruch began his 1932 foreword to *Popular Delusions* by telling us that "all economic movements, by their very nature, are motivated by crowd psychology." This is a truism, but it's magnified today because the crowd has grown much bigger than at any time in the history of the human species. When Baruch wrote his foreword, it was during the depths of the Great Depression. This must have been a time of deep and total despair for many, yet humankind always seems to muddle through the bad times, as he so sagely concluded we would at that time: "Similarly, even in this general moment of gloom in which this foreword is written, when many begin to wonder if declines will never halt, the appropriate abracadabra may be: 'They always did.'"

George Kleinman
Lake Tahoe, Nevada
September 2008

chapter 1

Eliminating People

"Most of the world's ills would be cured with one three-day open season on people."
–Ernest Hemingway

"They're not just getting rich...they're getting even."
–*Trading Places* (1983)

An electric tension fills the air as Louis Winthorpe, III and Billy Ray Valentine muscle their way through the crowd of traders lining the New York Board of Trade's frozen concentrated orange juice (FCOJ) trading pit. The traders are sweating from the heat generated by more than 100 tightly packed bodies, nervous with the anticipation of what's to come. The clerks manning the phones surrounding the pit are on high alert.

The crop report will be released in just minutes. When those numbers are out, the market will move big time, creating and destroying fortunes in the process.

Winthorpe and Valentine are now standing shoulder to shoulder with other traders eyeing their arch nemesis—the ultimate slime ball, Clarence Beeks. Beeks believes he already knows the actual crop report numbers. He illegally obtained an advance copy of the report in his quest to corner the orange juice market on behalf of the infamous Duke Brothers. However, our heroes learned of Beeks's plan: They managed to steal the real crop report back from Beeks and secretly delivered him a fake version.

The "real" crop report will show a record-large orange harvest, resulting in huge supplies that will ultimately cause the traders to yell "Sell!" Beeks believes the numbers in his false report and will be looking for the orange crop numbers to be sharply lower. He is planning to "Buy!" in his quest to corner the orange juice market for the Dukes.

Futures are traded on margin, with only a small deposit required to purchase a large amount of an asset. It's just as easy to short—to sell first and then buy back later (hopefully lower)—as it is to be a buyer. Commodities can be very volatile, particularly on crop report day.

The opening bell rings and immediately the decibel level explodes. All trades in the pit are made by the "open outcry" process where the traders yell out their bids and offers. Beeks starts hitting all offers, screaming "Buy, buy, buy!" Most of the traders in the pit are merely sheep looking to hop on for the ride. Seeing Beeks bidding the market up, they believe he knows something and join in his buying frenzy. The rumors have started to fly: "The Duke Brothers (with Beeks as their agent) are looking to corner the market!"

FCOJ prices are now on a tear, rising as high as $1.45 per pound. Until now, Winthorpe and Valentine have been lying in the weeds and with perfect timing begin to scream "Sell, sell, sell!" right at the top of the market. The true crop report numbers are then revealed, and the market begins to crash and, once again, at the optimal low point of 29¢ per pound, our boys reverse course and start screaming "Buy, buy, buy!" They are now covering their short sales. The majority of these sales were made—well above $1 per pound, so they are covering from 25¢ to 46¢ and netting millions in the process. The Dukes, having bought near the top, are left holding the bag.

The classic 1983 comedy *Trading Places* is one of my all-time favorites. Winthorpe is beautifully portrayed by Dan Aykroyd as a rich commodity broker turned homeless, with Valentine played by the comic genius Eddie Murphy as a homeless man transformed into a rich commodity broker. Many people believe that the story was inspired by the silver market's incredible rise and ultimate fall in 1980 when the Hunt brothers of Texas tried unsuccessfully to corner that market. Silver prices crashed in March of that year when the brothers were unable to meet their last $100 million margin call.

The unsung star of *Trading Places* was the trading pit itself—the actual pit at the New York Board of Trade (NYBOT) where real traders played themselves in the movie. The climactic scene (in most viewers' minds) is the chaotic buying frenzy that took place in the pit (although some male viewers might argue the climactic scene was when Jamie Lee Curtis took her sweater off). In any case, the movie would not have been as visually exciting or nearly as suspenseful without the trading pit. It's hard to imagine any excitement if our heroes were just clicking a mouse in front of a computer screen.

Trading Places is now more than 25 years old. The NYBOT—the exchange where coffee, cocoa, sugar, and, yes, FCOJ is traded—was established in 1870. Here comes the sad part: On December 13, 2007, the NYBOT board of directors voted unanimously to permanently close the trading floor, moving 100% of the commodities trading to the computer screen. Open-outcry trading, the backbone of the Exchange for more than 100 years, was permanently silenced in February 2008. It was progress, but the pit closing put 1,000 traders and support staff out of work. One veteran pit trader told a *New York Post* reporter, "Most of these people really don't know how to do anything else, and now we will all have to find our place in the world." However, other than these folks, the closing had little to no effect on the dealings in these key global commodities. That's because more than 90% of the volume had already moved to the computer screen by this time. In the rest of the world, electronic trading for commodities had been the norm for years. Although small pockets of pit traders remain in certain commodities, the writing's on the wall. The computer will ultimately totally eliminate the pit trader. Why? Pure economics—it's cheaper. No need for traders to leave their homes in the morning. No need to maintain a downtown facility with the associated high rents and utility costs. No need to hire runners, phone clerks, and trading clerks. And above all, no need for the pit trader. I used to pay a good pit trader an extra $2–$5 per contract (above normal clearing fees) to execute my trades, and I was glad to do so. If the guy was louder or bigger or quicker than my competitor's floor broker, I would often get the better price.

The cost savings of computerized trading is obvious, but another advantage emerges: a level playing field. Ernest Hemingway once said, "The best way to find out if you can trust somebody is to trust them." In the olden days, you really had to trust your pit broker. Let me share a true story with you. Years ago, I was using a floor broker in the New York silver pit to execute my trades there. All was going well until one day I placed an order to buy 50 silver contracts at a price that should have been easily filled. After some time had elapsed, the market surged higher, netting me a tidy profit—or, at least, that's what I thought. I had been waiting for the pit broker's phone clerk to call me back with the fill. He hadn't called yet, so I called the floor. The broker got on the phone and denied I had ever placed the order. To this day, I have little doubt that he filled the order and pocketed my profit for himself. Because the phone call wasn't recorded at that time, my only recourse was to never use this guy again, and subsequently I did find a pit broker I could trust. This kind of problem doesn't occur with electronic trading—the computer can't lie.

Other than the substantial cost savings of eliminating people, electronic trading offers additional benefits. You can place orders faster, as fast as a mouse click. During a fast-moving market in the olden days, it was entirely possible to miss our price by the time the runner delivered our order to the pit broker. Even with using a market order (required to be filled at the next available price) during a wild pit session, we might not have known for hours what price we were filled at. In erratic market conditions, a good fill was often the luck of the draw. Today these doubts are gone—fills return to the trader instantaneously. The computer can also manage multiple orders and price fills more efficiently than a human. Clearing firms like computerized trading as well because credit and risk management is automated. The computer can cut off an out-of-control trader before the trader's account ever moves into an unsecured debit position.

Reduced cost, speed, enhanced information management, the expansion of markets globally with 24-hour trading...isn't technology terrific? Other than the loss of a few jobs and the romanticism of the bygone era of the pits, are there any downsides?

The legendary trader Jesse Livermore once said something to the effect that technology might change, but the markets never will because markets are made by human beings and human nature doesn't change. Traders today still make the same mistakes made by traders 50 or 100 years ago. This is true. Markets will continue to trend up and trend down.

"The trend is your friend" was a basic theme of my previous books. This truism has not changed and will remain a primary theme for successful trading in this book. I can cite literally thousands of examples of markets that have trended long and far and, in the process, made some people rich and wiped out many others. You might have heard about the poor soul who lost his farm. I can almost guarantee that guy was bull-headed and fought the prevailing trend of the market until he finally ran out of money.

In the 1920s, the New Haven railroad was the premier blue-chip stock of the day and sold as high as $279 per share. In those days, you could trade stocks on 5% margin as we trade futures today. When New Haven sold 50 points off the top, it must have looked cheap at the time. How many would have had the guts to sell it short when it crossed below 179, 100 points from the top? Better yet, who would have had the guts, or the vision, to sell this investment-grade security short at 79, or 200 points from the top? It must have looked extremely cheap at 79—remember, this was the Apple or GE of its day. Yet the trend was down, and after the crash of 1929, it traded as low as 12. In 2000, a friend of mine bought a "new technology" stock at the offering price of $66. He added to his position at $150 a share, again at $200, and then again at $300. I suggested he use stops to lock in his profit, but he "knew" this company was only going up (his daughter worked there), and he told me it would ultimately trade at $1,000. It did keep going up beyond what I imagined it ever could, and he added to his position at $450 and $500. It actually traded as high as $600. Today it has ceased trading, going off the board at $0.

Remember Enron? This was a "blue-chip" energy company and the largest contributor to the 2000 Bush presidential campaign. At that time, the stock was trading at $90 a share. Today it no longer exists. If you still own the stock, you can use your certificate as wallpaper. *The trend is your friend—do not fight it.* Electronic trading will not eliminate trends or eliminate future Enrons or silver crashes. The keys to successful trading are still, and always will be, successfully identifying the trend and practicing good money management, combined with the essential qualities of patience and discipline.

I have long subscribed to Livermore's belief that markets do not change because human nature does not change. In many ways, this is a truism, but not in one major way. Eliminating people from the middle of the equation *has* made a big difference. Electronic trading *has* changed the markets—hence the reason for this book. As a trader, I've had to adjust to new market realities. And if you trade commodities, you absolutely will need to adjust your methods as well. One of the objectives of this book is to help guide you through these uncharted waters.

What are the consequences of eliminating people? The answer, in one word, is *volatility*. As a result, new trading skills are required for success. Speed and volume have combined to make the markets more volatile. Volatility can lead to trader anxiety; however, an anxious trader will not be a successful trader. Succeeding in trading today requires the ability to cope with exploding volatility. Think I exaggerate here? At times the markets have always been volatile, right?

Are you old enough to remember the good old days when gasoline was less than $1 a gallon? Consider Chart 1.1.

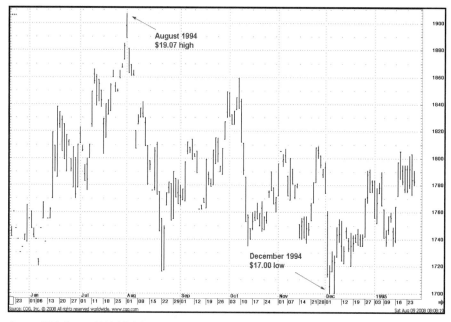

Chart 1.1   Crude oil 1994–1995

This is a daily chart of the oil market for the 1994–1995 trading period. Each vertical line represents one full day of trading. You are looking at nearly one full year of oil futures trading. The chart appears to illustrate a volatile market with big ups and downs throughout this period. However, it all depends on how the chart is scaled.

The price range during this ten-month period was an extreme high of $19.07 per barrel in August, with an extreme low of $17 in December. This is a $2.07-per-barrel range from high to low within this entire period. The size of one oil futures contract is 1,000 barrels; therefore, every $1-per-barrel move equals $1,000 profit or loss per contract traded. During this 12-month period, we saw approximately a $2,000-per-contract range in price movement between the two extremes—not an atypical year for that period.

Today the oil contract size is exactly the same; however, volatility has exploded. Consider this recent example in Chart 1.2.

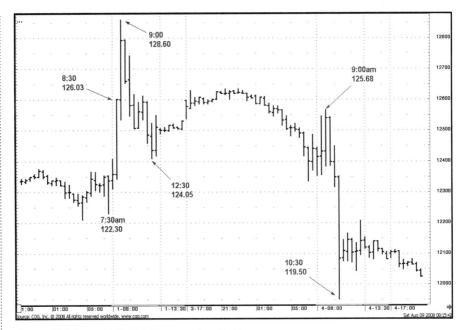

Source: CQG, Inc. © 2008 All rights reserved worldwide.

Chart 1.2 Two days of oil trading

You're now looking at a 30-minute chart of the oil market that covers just two days in August 2008. Each vertical line represents 30 minutes of trading (versus one day per line in the previous chart). During the first highlighted one-hour period (two 30-minute bars), the price ranged from $122.30 per barrel to $126.03 per barrel, and *in just one additional 30-minute period* (from 8:30 a.m. to 9:30 a.m. CST), oil ran up an additional $2.57. Within just this 1 1/2-hour period, the range was $6.30, or $6,300 per contract traded. In only 90 minutes this day, the price range was triple of the entire 1994–1995 trading year. The next day, a similar dollar move *in the exact opposite direction* occurred. This is not atypical for the current market environment.

How about this? Chart 1.3 is a one-minute chart of the soybean market. Each vertical bar represents one minute of trading.

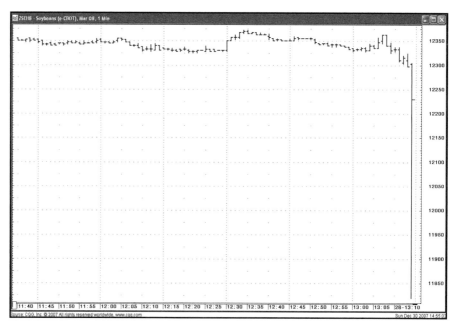

Chart 1.3   One-minute soybean chart

Seemingly out of nowhere in a quiet market, the beans collapsed 50¢ a bushel and then immediately recovered, all in less than one minute. This is equivalent to a $2,500 move per contract *down and back up in less than a minute.* Today, action such as this is unfortunately (or fortunately) quite common.

Why this dramatic rise in volatility? Screen trading is the major culprit; however, reasons other than electronic trading are to blame, too. Commodity demand has multiplied in recent years due to the dramatic industrial revolution in a number of countries, notably China. This demand increase (with a dose of inflation) has resulted in higher prices. Higher prices lead to larger ranges for the same percentage moves. For $19 oil, a 10% move equals $1.90, but for $90 oil, a 10% move equals $9. So this is part of it, but it doesn't fully explain the velocity and ferocity of today's market movements (let alone the volatility).

Remember the old days when you heard a song on the radio and wanted to buy the album? The process involved physically going to the record store, finding what you were looking for, and returning home to play it. This process took time. Now you can find and download music in seconds over the Internet.

The main reason for the increased speed of market movements is the Internet—a direct result of the dramatic shift during the past few years away from nearly 100% pit trading to nearly 100% electronic trading.

Until recently, this is the way I would place an order in the commodity markets: I would pick up the phone and dial a trading floor. Hopefully, the clerk would pick up the phone call in a timely manner, but in a fast-moving market, sometimes it would ring forever, and this could be maddening. When the clerk did pick up the call, I would read my order, and the clerk would write it on an order ticket and then time-stamp the ticket. Good procedure required the clerk to read back my order to me for confirmation and consistency before he or she sent it off. The clerk would then pass my order to a runner (hopefully the runner was near the phone clerk and not out having a cigarette), who then physically walked it to my broker in the trading pit (or, at times, the broker's clerk adjacent to him in the pit). The pit broker would cue the order, and when the market approached my price, he or she would yell out the buy or sell into the trading pit, looking for an offsetting trade via the open-outcry process. After it was filled, the process would reverse from runner to clerk, with more time stamps, and eventually it would be phoned back to me. This all took time. Looking back, it is amazing we operated this way, in most cases efficiently, for the bulk of my trading career.

Now with electronic trading, orders are disseminated and received instantly over the Internet. Orders of all sizes from around the globe are now entered instantly with a mouse click, eliminating this entire human-based process.

This volatility enables many opportunities, but it also increases the risk geometrically compared to the old days. So how does a trader cope with this rise in volatility? The answer lies in computing power. We used to keep charts by hand, but now the computer draws the charts for us. A computer also calculates those same market studies in real time that we used to do at night by hand after the market closed.

As an example, in Chart 1.4, I've reproduced the 30-minute oil chart and superimposed a 60-period simple moving average. By monitoring where the market is in relation to this average (particularly on a close for each period), the computer can help a trader identify the true internal trend of a market. Today a trader needs to compress his time parameters and use computing power over shorter time spans. The computer cannot eliminate the volatility and speed of today's markets—these factors are here to stay. But computing power in today's market environment is a necessity to analyze the markets at a speed the human brain is incapable of doing.

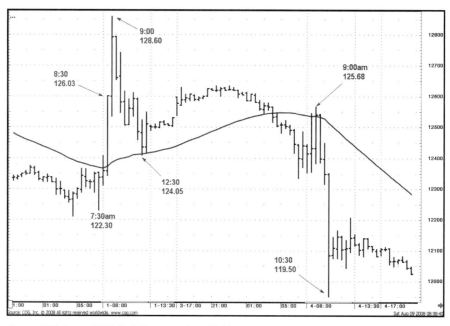

Source: CQG, Inc. © 2008 All rights reserved worldwide.

Chart 1.4   Thirty-minute chart (with moving average)

The bottom line of the market change is that electronics speed up the process, resulting in greater volatility. This means that, as traders, we also need to change and use technology while maintaining those time-tested methods that work.

The objective of this book is to meld the necessary adjustments for the current market environment while maintaining those timeless methodologies that have worked in the past and will continue to work in the future because of human nature. Fear and greed ultimately move markets. And no matter what machines we utilize, these human traits will never go away. Speed can be our friend or our enemy. As the legendary trader W. D. Gann once wrote, "Most people are in too big a hurry to get rich and as a result they go broke."

chapter 2

Capturing a 5,000% Return

"How do we know when irrational exuberance has unduly escalated asset values?"
—Alan Greenspan (1996)

A variety of commodity markets have made historic price moves in recent years—moves that couldn't have been imagined before the advent of electronic trading and the economic rise of the newly developed nations.

This chapter explores a remarkable story of one of these virtually "impossible" market moves that theoretically returned 5,000% on margin—in just three months.

Even the sleaziest of investment scam artists wouldn't promise returns of this magnitude, after all, this number sounds fairly ridiculous. Yet this seemingly impossible move was quite real. Even more remarkable is that this phenomenal annualized return of 20,000% isn't being measured from the theoretical bottom to the top. Before this all began, the market in question had *already* doubled in price.

This event took place in a market not generally known for big moves at the low-volume, sometimes sleepy, smallest U.S futures marketplace: the Minneapolis Grain Exchange (MGE).

This is the story of one of the most incredible price moves to take place in the history of markets. I lived through this story with two clients: one who was on the right side and one who wasn't. The guy on the right side saw his account grow by seven figures, and the guy on the wrong side saw his account decrease by a similar amount. This is a story of greed, stubbornness, and vision. Looking back, the market telegraphed all the crystal clear signals that a trader needed to know (both fundamentally and technically) to be on the right side of it. In hindsight, it appeared easy to profit, but then again, it's never easy, and hindsight is always 20/20. By reviewing what happened here, we can learn how to more effectively trade markets such as this in the future.

This is the remarkable story of the Minneapolis wheat market of 2007–2008:

Three major varieties of wheat are traded on the U.S. exchanges. The most plentiful variety is hard-winter wheat traded in Kansas City. This type of wheat is used for bread and is grown primarily in Kansas, Texas, and Oklahoma. The Chicago variety is soft-winter wheat, used for cakes and pastries, and grown primarily in Missouri and Illinois. The spring variety that's traded at the MGE is primarily grown in North Dakota, but also South Dakota, Montana, and Minnesota. Unlike the winter varieties, as its name implies, spring wheat is planted in the spring and harvested in late summer. It's a premium, higher-protein variety used in baked goods such as bagels, French bread, and hard rolls. All three are the same globally traded commodity but are different varieties that generally move in the same direction, however, at varying speeds.

In 2007, the world experienced widespread wheat production problems due to devastating heat stress in Europe, Australia, Russia, and the Black Sea region. The result was that all wheat prices in all three markets rose dramatically throughout the second half of the year.

Anticipating the big move to come, the Minneapolis wheat futures formed a head and shoulders bottom formation in early June, completed when the market broke above $5.50 per bushel. In all my trading years, I've found the head and shoulders to be one of the two most powerful classic chart patterns. The second is the breakout from a consolidation; both are consolidation breakout patterns. (These two patterns have been around since charts were invented. Because they remain so reliable, I've devoted the next chapter to them. If you're not familiar with how to identify and trade these patterns, consider reading Chapter 3, "Two Chart Patterns That Work," now.)

On the daily 2007 Minneapolis wheat chart (Chart 2.1), I've identified the breakout from the neckline of a clear head and shoulders consolidation pattern. This breakout in early June completed a major bottom formation and projected a minimum move to somewhere above the $6 level. In actuality, it jumpstarted a much bigger move than that, with a sharp rally up to the $9 per bushel level by late September, before the first $1 correction. This move from $5.50 to $9 was, in itself, quite dramatic—the dollar equivalent of a $17,500 move on just one 5,000-bushel contract.

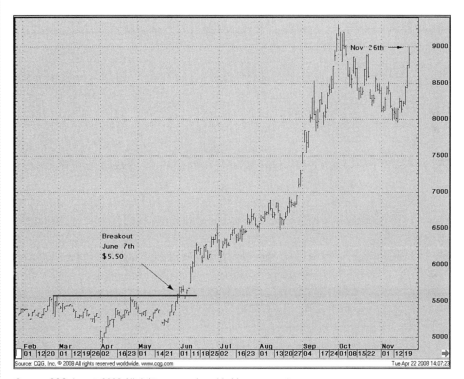

Chart 2.1   2007 Minneapolis wheat

High prices generally lead to increased production and lower prices. However, in the world's biggest wheat exporter, the United States, the winter wheat crop (planted in the fall for a summer harvest) was a poor one. In addition, the protein content of the winter crop was low, and this is important to our story because it placed additional pressure on the spring wheat crop to replenish supplies of high-protein wheat. However, the wheat farmers in North Dakota and Minnesota, lured by the new biofuels promise of potentially higher corn and soybean prices, actually planted record acres of those crops and reduced their spring-wheat acres.

After the spring planting, the summer growing weather in the Dakotas was less than ideal. The lower acres combined with poor yields resulted in a short spring-wheat crop. Add this to the tight world supplies, and these events combined to create the lowest level of world wheat supplies in more than 60 years. In 2007–2008, the global supply of wheat as a percentage of usage was just 18%, the lowest number since World War II. This scenario created an even greater demand for the already short Minneapolis variety—a perfect market storm. Not only did smaller supplies and greater demand result in a sharp gain in the Minneapolis futures prices, but Minneapolis (high-protein spring) wheat also gained dramatically *in relation* to the already high prices for the Chicago and Kansas City varieties. Although millers can substitute different wheat varieties for many applications, spring wheat is required in the blending of higher-protein bread types, and it's the variety most prized by the Japanese (who import most of their spring wheat from the United States).

Prices continued rising into early 2008, reaching a new all-time high of $11 per bushel in January. The high prices didn't appear to deter most buyers; during February, the Japanese entered the marketplace with a standard weekly tender for 80,000 tons of spring wheat. Even though prices were at all-time highs (with every economic incentive for farmers to clean out their bins), the Japanese received offers for only 50,000 tons. This was a wake-up call to wheat traders, who started believing that the United States was totally sold out of spring wheat. The message was, "No spring wheat left, with six months until the next crop became available." The result was a classic buying panic. Prices soared in a parabolic move higher, surging to the truly incredible price of $24 per bushel by the end of February.

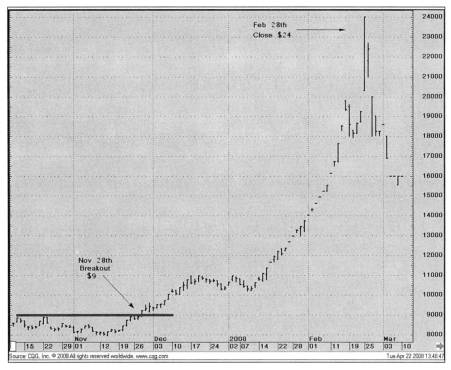

Source: CQG, Inc. © 2008 All rights reserved worldwide.

Chart 2.2   March 2008 Minneapolis wheat

It's tough to put these numbers in their proper perspective, but let me try.

Until 2007, the all-time high price for Minneapolis wheat was $7.23 per bushel, reached briefly in May 1996. The price then broke back to less than $4 per bushel after the new crop became available a few months later. For the seven years following 1996, wheat prices didn't go over that $4 per bushel. For the majority of those years, it was rare to see a $1-per-bushel move for an entire year. In contrast, the price of spring wheat in February 2008 moved more than $4 per bushel in just one week.

In late 2007, the margin deposit to trade one contract of spring wheat on the MGE was $1,350, a new all-time high. As the market moved higher, the MGE eventually raised margins to $7,150 per contract. What do these numbers mean in real dollars? A futures contract for Minneapolis wheat is a standard size— 5,000 bushels. Therefore, every penny-per-bushel movement in price is equivalent to a $50 profit or loss per contract traded. Margin in futures is similar to a good-faith deposit and is returned to the trader when he exits, plus any profits or minus any losses. Therefore, a "limit move" of 30¢ adds the equivalent of

$1,500 per contract to the trader's account on the right side and subtracts this amount from the player on the wrong side.

At the beginning of 2008, the March contract was trading at the then all-time unbelievably high price of $10 per bushel. This was double, up $5 per bushel from early 2007. Just one contract returned the equivalent of $25,000 on this $5 move.

The next move, from $10 to $24, represents an incredible and additional $70,000 profit (or loss) for just one contract and in only a few months. The $5 move on February 28 alone equaled $25,000 on just a single contract. A $70,000 profit on a $1,350 margin deposit for one contract equals a 5,185% return in only three months.

Now imagine being on the wrong side of this move, thinking prices at "you pick the number" were just too high. Anyone who thinks that he or she has deep enough pockets to ride out moves similar to this on the wrong side should heed the words of the great economist John Maynard Keynes: "The market can stay irrational longer than you can stay solvent."

During this drama in the futures, around the globe wheat buyers paid more for a premium loaf of bread or a kaiser roll (both of which use high-protein wheat). This brings up the question of who benefits from a price move such as this. In addition to the traders on the right side of the market, feel good for those farmers who held on to some of their production from the 2007 crop and sold in the upper double-digits—they were big winners. However, only a few farmers were in that group because, in the nature of a market such as this, the great majority of farmers had sold out their wheat inventories months earlier. After all, wouldn't you take that $10 per bushel in January, the highest price ever seen in history to that date? And that's the basic reason only a dearth of spring wheat existed in the first quarter of 2007.

This price move in Minneapolis wheat was unprecedented, and although a big move still would have occurred, it would not have happened to this extent in the days of fewer people, fewer hedge funds, and pit-traded (versus electronic) markets. To cope with the volatility, the Minneapolis Grain Exchange put into place a new limit policy. Price limits for nearly 100 years were restricted to 20¢ per bushel per day. In 1998, the MGE raised the limits to 30¢, and it stayed at that number for ten years until February 2008. Because of the mayhem, the MGE not only doubled the daily limit to 60¢, but it also instituted an expanding-limit policy. Today, if the MGE market closes at the 60 limit, it can increase to 90 the next day, then 135, and then 202.5, based on a formula contingent on how the market traded the day before. Then on a certain date, the MGE removes the limit on the spot month entirely. Nobody could even imagine doing this in the olden days.

At the price peak, grain merchandisers were scouring five states in search of spring wheat and couldn't find any. The price for a bushel of spring wheat was whatever was demanded. However, at the end of this story, the day the world theoretically ran out of spring wheat was actually the day the highs were made. In 1928, the great trader W. D. Gann made the following observation: "The history of the world shows that there never has been a time when there was a great demand for anything, whether it be a product of the mine, factory, or farm, that sooner or later a supply in excess of that demand did not develop. This is but a natural law."

The March 2008 contract that traded as high as $24 per bushel went off the board at $17. The trade for actual cash spring wheat dried up the first half of 2008, and by May, prices were back down to $11 per bushel—despite the fact that not one additional bushel of spring wheat had been grown since the highs were made. In the end, it wasn't a question of supplies increasing; instead, we now know that demand had become totally satiated. Bakers switched to lower-protein wheat where they could, and some consumers balked at paying $1 for one bagel. But the real reason prices went down was that the Japanese (and others) paid increasingly more in a frenzy to secure supplies until their demand was satiated. These buyers were afraid they would run out, so they went on a panicked buying streak and effectively bought their entire needs for the year in February. This action created the parabolic-type move and the panic-induced high price. Millers were still working through $20 wheat in their storage facilities when wheat was trading back down at $10. Bottom line: When the panic buying dried up, prices plummeted.

A trader can learn three major lessons from this example, with lesson number one being the most important:

1. Never fight the trend—"the trend is your friend." This is especially true during major uptrends. Who could have forecast oil at $147 per barrel when it was $60 the year before? I could give you a list three pages long of markets that moved far higher than anyone had thought possible, with another list of bankrupt nonbelievers filling a book. (This lesson is so important that Chapter 8, "The Trend Is Your Friend," is devoted to it.)

2. What's important is not the news, but how the market reacts to the news. This is especially true when a market fails to continue with a bull move after the bullish news is out. Certainly, the news sets the public perception, but you must be alert for divergences between the news and market action. It's expectation versus reality. Look for the divergence between what's happening and what people think is supposed to happen. When the big

turn comes, the general public (and even astute insiders) will always be looking the wrong way.

You can analyze reactions to news (or even a lack of news) in three ways:

- Moves of importance invariably tend to begin before any news justifies the initial price move. When the move is underway, the emerging fundamentals will slowly come to light.

- A big rally (decline) on *no news* is usually very bullish (bearish). The 2007 wheat bull market was well underway before the world realized how critical the situation had become.

- It is generally not a good practice to buy after a lot of very bullish news or sell after an extremely bearish report, because both good and bad news is usually already discounted in the price.

(Chapter 6, "The Significant News Indicator," presents an indicator to help you profitably trade news.)

3. Panic markets usually seem to top out in the same way. When close to the end of a major move, markets tend to become wild. Volume is huge, activity is feverish and erratic, and the imagination of most traders blossoms. If you've had the vision to ride the trend to this point, your payday has come. However, in extreme markets, people of reason lose all sense of proportion. They start to believe the propaganda that the world has literally run out of this food or that metal, but it never happens. In the late 1970s, the Hunts ran silver from $5 an ounce to more than $50. They felt it would go up forever, but they forgot that at some price, Grandma's silver candlesticks come out of the cupboard and are sent to the smelter. The richest men in the world (at that time) lost all sense of reason and proportion, losing $2 billion in the process.

Always remember what Gann told us: "The history of the world shows that there never has been a time when there was a great demand for anything, whether it be a product of the mine, factory, or farm, that sooner or later a supply in excess of that demand did not develop. This is but a natural law."

chapter 3

Two Chart Patterns That Work

"Stupidity got us into this mess, and stupidity will get us out!"
—Homer Simpson

Shortly I introduce new trading methodologies for the new electronic age, but in the spirit of not throwing out the baby with the bathwater, let's begin with what still works. In the previous chapter, I mentioned what I believe are the two most powerful classic chart patterns that continue to work.

Many people are skeptical that a chart pattern can lead to profitability. Being human, people need logical explanations for why a market moves in a certain direction. The fundamentals of supply and demand provide that logical explanation. The problem for the trader is that the explanation is often presented in the past tense.

How do you define a fundamental? In the words of George Soros, perhaps the world's premier fund manager, the most important fundamental is *money flow.* How often has the oil inventory report come out bearish but the market closed higher? In both the short and the long run, money flow is most important to market direction—that is, are the buyers or the sellers more aggressive? Chart patterns can help answer this question.

Global commodity consuming and producing firms possess the resources to gather timely and accurate fundamental data. This information is not enough by itself to guarantee profitability, but this investment in market intelligence suggests that their information is better than what the rest of us are getting. Nestlé makes it the company's business to know how the cocoa crop in the Ivory Coast is developing. You and I might read a brokerage house report that discusses the "witch's tail disease" and how it has the potential to devastate the crop, but Nestlé has its people in the Ivory Coast, with others in Brazil, walking the fields. They have a better feel for how good or bad the crops look than we'll ever have, and they have no reason or obligation to share this information with the rest of us. Suppose the cocoa crop is actually deteriorating. A confidential communiqué would be wired to Switzerland, and those in charge of cocoa purchasing for Nestlé would get busy. One aspect of their job is to hedge by buying cocoa futures. If the odds favor a drop in supply, odds favor prices rising *after* the news is known. The purpose of a hedge is to protect against future price risk. The Nestlé traders will attempt to hedge by accumulating cocoa futures as quietly as possibly before you or I know what they are up to. But there's a catch. No entity is able to place a large position in a freely traded market, either on the long or the short side, without leaving what I call "footprints in the sand." Large, significant, "informed" volume must be reported according to Exchange rules, and volume will inevitably move price. Technical analysis is about analyzing current price action and comparing it to past price action to project future price action.

Does it really work? My 30 years of trading experience says it does. Solid technical analysis is perhaps the only tool that can give the individual trader a decent chance against the professionals. You might not have the research capabilities of the commercial firms, but you do have the luxury of moving faster than the big commercial operators because your trading size will not affect price significantly. You are not stuck trading just one market (which might not be moving). You can relax in the comfort of your home or office and analyze your charts.

Pure technicians believe that the most important factor in predicting the markets is *price action*. They don't look at crop size, export data, trade imbalances, or employment numbers. They don't care if it's raining in Brazil or if the head of the European Central Bank just made a speech hinting at an interest rate rise. Technicians primarily care about price action.

This is not to say that technicians don't believe fundamentals move the markets. They concede this fact. A technician might know that soybean prices are rising because drought is devastating the Brazilian crop, but he or she will also tell you that price will signal when the diminished supply has finally been rationed by diminished demand—and this could happen long before the drought has broken.

The technician believes that all the pertinent fundamental information, perhaps hundreds of bits of data impossible for any mortal to assimilate, will be reflected in price and price action. In essence, the price action will reflect the consensus of the market players far better than the mainstream fundamental information available to the public trader. With this in mind, let's look at two classic chart patterns that possess significant predictive qualities: the breakout and the head and shoulders (H&S).

The Breakout from Consolidation

Think of a market bouncing off "support" similar to a ball bouncing off the floor. If the floor is a deck four stories off the ground, it will bounce as long it remains on the deck. But if it subsequently falls off the deck, it drops lower. Alternatively, "resistance" is similar to a ceiling, but if a glass ceiling is smashed, the birds are free to fly higher.

Support and resistance levels are very important to traders. When a market is in a relatively flat range (holding at support *and* failing at resistance), it's called *consolidation*. Consolidation is an inability by either the bulls or the bears to win the battle. When the market holds at some level, rallies, and then again retreats to that same level, it then appears cheap. Those bulls that missed the first rally feel as if they have a second chance at "cheap" levels and step up to the plate. The shorts, especially those who are scalping and selling at higher levels, see the market start to bounce, and they're induced to cover their shorts before their paper profits disappear. This additional buying—short covering—adds fuel to the bull move. The reverse occurs when the market rallies to the level of previous failure—the resistance point. Some of the longs who previously purchased at support might feel that the market is looking expensive and cash in. Bears, who missed selling the last rally, will consider this a "second chance" and start selling. The market starts its retreat, and other longs (who do not want to see their paper profits disappear) sell out, adding fuel to the bear fire. We know that if a market fails at a resistance level on numerous occasions and over a significant period of time, and then proceeds to trade above that level, this is a sign that the bears have lost the battle. The buying interest was finally strong enough to overwhelm the selling interest, and the defensive ceiling built by the bears has been shattered. (The opposite is happening if a support level is broken.) In simpler terms, a break above resistance or below support indicates that a major shift is probably taking place in the supply and demand fundamentals of the market in question. Chart 3.1 shows what a breakout looks like graphically.

Take a look at the 1988 oats chart shown in Chart 3.2: the monster oats rally that drove prices to all-time highs that were not exceeded for the following 20 years. Look at how long and beautiful the consolidation was that preceded this bull move.

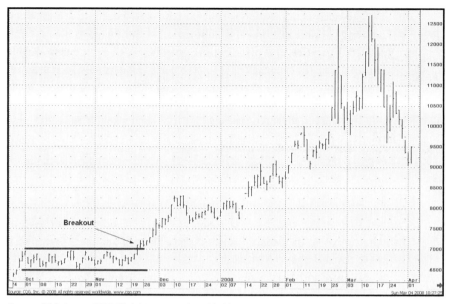

Chart 3.1   Soybean breakout

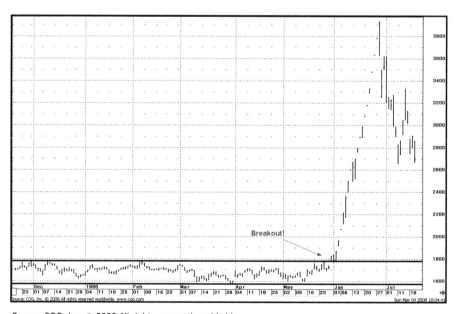

Chart 3.2   July 1988 oats

Those of you who have read my previous book *Trading Commodities and Financial Futures* know that I have a soft spot in my heart for this 1988 oats move. Consider the following true story:

I had a wealthy client who was stubborn and gutsy, and who would not get out of his March 1988 oats contract because he felt they were too cheap. He had two million bushels (the limit an individual could own at that time), and I told him that if he didn't get out, he would get delivery. I liked the oat market but suggested that he roll his March contracts into July. No, he told me he would take the delivery—even though when delivery takes place, a trader is required to put up the full value of the contract and is no longer on margin. So he took delivery of the two million bushels at approximately $1.60 per bushel in March. He wired the $3,200,000. From that day on, he told me that my job was to look for a good bid to sell the oats in the cash market, but neither of the big boys (General Mills nor Quaker Oats) seemed interested. The market traded in the consolidation range for a few months, and then it got hot and dry. (That's what caused the breakout from the long consolidation you see in Chart 3.2.)

The drought of 1988 is history now, but let me tell you the impact. The oat crop in the Dakotas was devastated. The futures traded up to approximately $4 per bushel. On June 28, the all-time record-high day for oats, I got a call from one of the large processors. He asked if the delivery oats were still for sale. I told him yes, and he promptly offered $4 per bushel for the entire two million. I called my client, who told me to reject the $4 bid and offer the whole lot at $4.40, "take it or leave it." When I called the processor back, he immediately said "Sold!" My client sold two million bushels of cash oats 40¢ per bushel higher than the futures price and at the all-time record price to that date. The client cleared a cool $5 million.

Months later, when I asked the grain man why he was so quick to buy the oats at a record-high price (remember, these are oats he didn't want at $1.60) of $4.40 (which was obviously too high based on the futures price), he told me this: "I had the choice of closing down the mill and putting 200 people out of work because I didn't have any oats to make oatmeal, or paying too much and bumping the price of a box of cereal by 10¢. What would you have done?"

These patterns are powerful and uncommon, and can occur in varying time frames. Let's look at a few other examples. The wheat example in Chart 3.3 illustrates a potentially false breakout (which later proved true) and the fact that breakouts from consolidations can occur during a trend move, not just at the beginning. I have found that a potentially "false" breakout, which later proves true via a successful second attempt, usually turns out to be an excellent signal. Certainly, these patterns can signify breakouts to the bear as well as the bull side, as the cattle example in Chart 3.4 illustrates.

Chart 3.3   2008 wheat

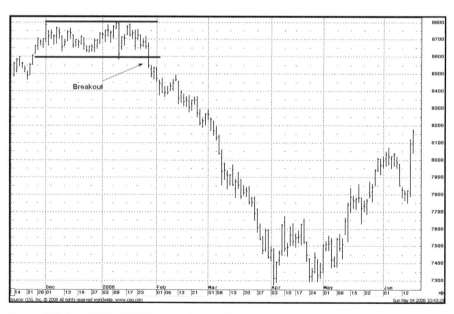

Chart 3.4   Cattle (downside breakout)

The previous charts are all daily charts (one bar equals one day's trading). In today's new electronic age, breakouts can occur in any time period, and traders need to be ready. Take a look at this breakout on the five-minute chart shown in Chart 3.5. (One bar on this chart equals five minutes of trading.)

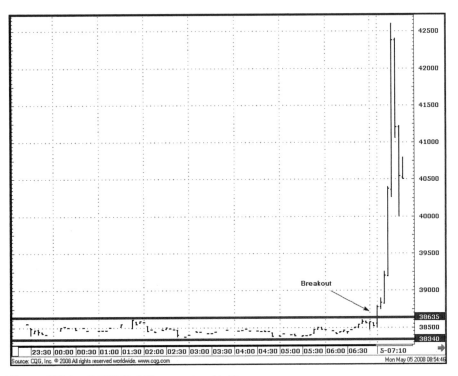

Source: CQG, Inc. © 2008 All rights reserved worldwide. www.cqg.com

Source: CQG, Inc. © 2008 All rights reserved worldwide.

Chart 3.5   Copper (five-minute chart)

On a sleepy Cinco de Mayo, with London closed due to a holiday, the New York copper market was in a tight consolidation between $3.83 and $3.86. The breakout above consolidation occurred at 7:10 AM above the $3.86 level. Within 20 minutes (four 5-minute bars on the chart), the market traded as high as $4.27, representing a move of 41¢, or $10,250 per contract. The margin for one contract at the time was $7,763, so this was more than a 100% return in less than a half-hour. Don't even try to calculate what the annualized return would look like—a ridiculous number. Ten minutes later, the market was back below $4. The news? There was none. Stops were hit all the way up, and the market eventually ended back where it started within a day. A move of this magnitude would not have occurred in this short of a time period during the pit days because professional pit traders would have stepped in to blunt the rally at an earlier stage. Still, the time-honored breakout from consolidation signaled the way to go on this one.

False Breakouts

Although this stuff is good, and I believe it usually works, you didn't think this would be all that easy, now, did you?

When I first discovered technical analysis, I studied the profitable examples in the books and thought this trading gig would be a piece of cake. Unfortunately, as with all of life, it doesn't work all the time. I must tell you that false breakouts from consolidation have occurred and will continue to occur. Many traders are well aware of how powerful a tool these patterns can be. As a result, they look for these breakouts. Many technicians will place stops just under support to limit losses or establish new short positions. Professional traders know intuitively where these stops will be. It's not sinister; they can make an educated guess on where the stops are by looking at a price chart, and they look at the same charts as everyone else. For example, if a market has held numerous times at 95 and it approaches that level again, what's to stop a professional trader from offering the market down to 94.90? The objective is to uncover the sell stops, and he can do this on the screen as well as he could have from the pit. A sell stop is a resting order to sell at some predetermined level. If the stops are actually "resting" at 94.90 (numerous brokers representing hundreds of traders from various unrelated firms could hold them), the selling commences.

Sometimes this action can feed on itself. The sell stops in place at 94.90 immediately begin to work. The resting orders to buy at 94.90 are filled, so the market is offered lower (94.80, 94.70, 94.60), but everyone seems to be selling, and its all on stops. The scalpers love this, especially in a quiet or thin market. They will come back in and bid at 94.50 and 94.40, for example, and cover their shorts at a quick and tidy profit. Because no fundamental substance caused this price action, the market quickly bounces back above 95 as the shorts are covered and commercial traders and bargain hunters step in. As a speculator, getting caught in a false breakout is frustrating. Seeing your stop hit and knock you out of a good position, only to watch the market quickly reverse in the direction you thought it was going in the first place, will steam you. If you trade long enough, this will happen to you, so keep your cool. Place your stops carefully, *where you don't think everyone else's stops are.*

Six Rules for Trading Breakouts from Consolidation

Breakouts from consolidation are such powerful indicators of potential trend changes that you should never become complacent when they occur just because false breakouts sometimes exist. My six rules for trading breakouts from consolidation should help.

1. The longer it takes to form a consolidation, the more significant the breakout and the bigger the expected move to follow. A breakout on a daily chart is more powerful than a 30-minute chart, and a breakout on a weekly chart is even more powerful. A breakout from consolidation on a yearly chart is the most powerful, signifying a major fundamental change in the supply-and-demand balance of that market.

2. After the breakout occurs, the market can retrace back to the breakout level, but it probably shouldn't trade back into the consolidation zone. If is does, the odds of a false breakout increase.

3. The breakout should remain above the breakout level for a significant amount of time. After it moves above the resistance or below the support, you shouldn't be in much trouble if you went with the breakout. If profits are not forthcoming in a reasonable amount of time, be wary. A *quick* failure is a symptom of a false breakout.

4. Watch the volume on the breakout day because a true breakout is generally associated with a sharp rise in the daily volume. Sometimes this high-volume level might precede the breakout by a day or two; however, false breakouts are usually associated with modest volume.

5. When trading a breakout using stops, never place your stops just below support or just above resistance. All the amateurs do this, and they become bait for running the stops. It's generally better to take a bit more risk and place your stop at a slightly greater distance.

6. A basic rule of thumb, which truly does work (if you use some judgment), is that when a market breaks out from consolidation, it will move roughly the distance up or down equal to the horizontal distance of the consolidation phase. I term this phenomenon "the count" (see Chart 3.6): *The longer the consolidation, the bigger the count.* To determine the count, measure the horizontal distance of the consolidation; then measure upward from the resistance breakout or downward from the support breakout, to give you an indication of the price objective for the coming move.

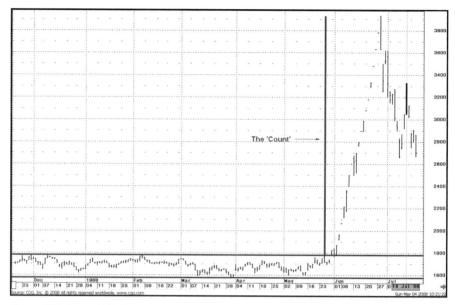

Chart 3.6   The count

The Head and Shoulders (H&S)

This chart pattern isn't new, but it's still really good. Robert D. Edwards and John Magee made the head and shoulders (H&S) pattern famous in their book *Technical Analysis of Stock Trends,* published in 1948. This book is often referred to as the "Bible of Technical Analysis." The basic premise was that prices of stocks and commodities move in repeating and identifiable patterns—the result of the ebb and flow of supply and demand. Although some of the concepts presented in the book were new at that time, many had been around since the turn of the century. The head and shoulders is one of those timeless patterns. Although markets have changed dramatically since the 1940s, human nature has not, so this pattern remains a valid indicator today.

The H&S is a reversal pattern, signaling a change in the prevailing major trend. I will spend time reviewing this concept because, in my experience, it remains one of the most reliable. I also add my own twist to identifying and analyzing this pattern. This pattern is also more common than the breakout from consolidation chart pattern discussed earlier.

When you see an H&S pattern, it's time to get out and take your profits, cut your losses, or establish a new position in the new direction. An interesting characteristic of the H&S is that it not only tells you a market is making a top or bottom, but it also tells you how far the ensuing move will travel. The H&S does not actually pick *the* top, or *the* bottom, but it gives you the sign after the top or bottom is in place.

Because a picture is worth a thousand words, let's start with a few charts that illustrate the H&S pattern. First consider Charts 3.7 and 3.8.

Source: CQG, Inc. © 2008 All rights reserved worldwide.

Chart 3.7   Sugar H&S top

Source: CQG, Inc. © 2008 All rights reserved worldwide.

Chart 3.8   Gold H&S top

The head (H) is a price peak; another peak lower than the head to the left is the left shoulder (LS), and another peak lower than the head to the right is the right shoulder (RS). The line connecting the lows of the declines from the shoulders and the head is called the neckline (NL). In a classic H&S, the neckline is often horizontal (similar to a support line). However, it can also be upward-sloping (as in Charts 3.7 and 3.8), similar to an uptrend line, or downward-sloping, similar to a downtrend line. This is where your analytical skills come into play. Many of the best H&S patterns are mutants, which resemble the original but in a skewed way.

You can spot an H&S developing when the left shoulder and the head are in place and the market starts to rally from the "neckline." If it fails at a lower high than the major high, the right shoulder is in formation. A classic H&S often has a right shoulder of the approximate same size and duration as the left. However, it can be lower or higher, longer or shorter, but its peak will ultimately end up lower than the head. The pattern is not complete until the right shoulder is completed *and* the decline from the right shoulder's peak breaks under the neckline. When that happens, a top is presumed. It is time to exit longs and go short. After the initial breakout below the neckline, the market often rallies back up to approximately the neckline, giving the trader an excellent low-risk shorting opportunity. H&S patterns can also sometimes provide false signals. Suspect a false signal if the market is able to rally back above the peak of RS. (This is the place to initially set your risk point.) This will not occur with the best H&S signals—most will not rally beyond the NL. If the market trades above the peak of the right shoulder, you can safely assume that all bets are off and this one isn't "right."

There's a bonus that comes with the H&S: It also provides a *target* that is generally reliable and more precise than most technical techniques. If you measure from the top of the head to the neckline and bring this measurement down from the neckline, you have a target for a *minimum objective* where prices will subsequently end up. The market can certainly move farther than this count for the objective, but it gives you a minimum objective that could prevent you from exiting prematurely.

H&S patterns occur in all time frames, and you can often find them in the short-term S&P chart. With a smaller pattern, you usually need to shoot for a smaller objective. Chart 3.9 illustrates a short-term complex H&S pattern on a 45-minute chart (each bar represents 45 minutes of market activity) that I traded successfully from the short side while I wrote this book.

Source: CQG, Inc. © 2008 All rights reserved worldwide.

Chart 3.9   Cocoa H&S

Watch volume to confirm the pattern. Volume often will tend to spike at the head and usually is higher than average at the break of the NL.

An H&S occurs at major bottoms as well and looks like the mirror image of one that forms at the top. Some traders call these *inverted head and shoulders,* or *reverse head and shoulders.* In this variety, the head is at the lowest point, with two higher shoulders at either side. Other than the fact that these are the mirror image of the tops, you trade them the same way. The gold H&S bottom (Chart 3.10) is of the simple, classic variety; the soybean illustration (Chart 3.11) is more complex. Note how the extended and complex bottoming pattern signaled the start of a major move that greatly exceeded the minimum objective (see rule 2).

Source: CQG, Inc. © 2008 All rights reserved worldwide.

Chart 3.10   Gold H&S bottom

Source: CQG, Inc. © 2008 All rights reserved worldwide.

Chart 3.11   Soybean H&S bottom (complex)

Ten Rules for Successfully Trading the Head and Shoulders

1. Never anticipate. When I first discovered H&S patterns, I had an excellent trade and then it seemed I started finding them everywhere. I would start to sell after a right shoulder and a head developed, only to lose money. I would see complete H&S patterns develop and take action *before* penetration of the neckline, only to have my head handed to me. As Yogi Berra said, "It ain't over till it's over." Wait until the pattern is completed before you trade it.

2. The bigger the H&S pattern and the longer it takes to develop, the bigger the subsequent resulting move.

3. The count is a *minimum* measurement. Odds actually favor the move carrying much further. However, a warning here: As with all chart patterns, we are not dealing with a certainty here. If your count says the market will fall 400 points, and it falls 380 and starts to reverse, it would be a shame to let all your profits evaporate over a lousy 20 points.

4. After the market breaks the neckline, watch for the return move back to the neckline. This occurs in at least half of all valid cases and offers a place to enter with a close stop.

5. Watch the slope of the neckline. Downward-sloping necklines for H&S tops increase the odds for a more powerful bear move to follow. Upward-sloping necklines for inverted H&S bottoms increase the odds for a more powerful bull move to follow.

6. Be volume cognizant. The most reliable neckline breakouts are accompanied with higher-than-average volumes. In retrospect, I have sometimes seen the highest daily volume days of the year associated with H&S patterns.

7. Watch for the head to also form an "island." This combines two very powerful patterns and geometrically increases the validity of the signal (see Chart 3.12).

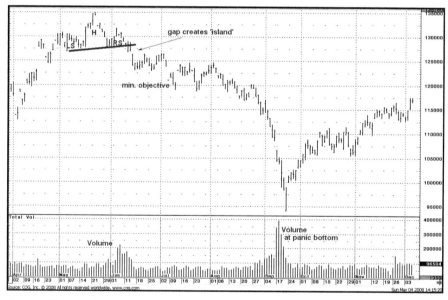

Source: CQG, Inc. © 2008 All rights reserved worldwide.

Chart 3.12   Island H&S top

8. When the pattern is completed, it should act correctly. These patterns are fairly reliable and do not often deviate from their true purpose, unless, of course, they are false. How can you tell if a pattern is false? One good indication is that your margin account will start to show a loss. Don't freeze when it's not acting properly—when in doubt, get out. Be suspicious if the pattern occurs on low volume. Remember, the market can retrace to the neckline—this is normal and a good place to position—but if the pattern is good, the retracement really shouldn't go much further.

9. If it's a false signal, look to reverse your course. I've found that a classic H&S failure often offers an excellent opportunity to get back in sync with the major trend. If the market again trades above the right shoulder's top (or below the right shoulder's bottom for a reverse H&S), odds favor, at the minimum, one last thrust to a new high or new low. I would buy the market at this point, with the objective of a new high, risking to under the neckline. For an inverted H&S failure, sell the market under the low of the right shoulder, with a minimum objective of a new low, risking to above the neckline.

10. After a false signal is confirmed, watch the market action closely as soon as a new high or low is registered. I've noticed that an H&S failure, not the final high or low, ultimately leads to a new contract high or low in short order. The H&S was telling us we were close to the major top or bottom, but the bulls or bears were able to mount one last hurrah. If the market is unable to show much follow-through after this climatic top or bottom (following an H&S that didn't work), be ready to take action because a major top or bottom is now in place.

chapter 4

The Voice from the Tomb (Super Seasonal #1)

"I'm not afraid of dying; I just don't want to be there when it happens."
—Woody Allen

When you have traded as long as I have, you acquire a lot of knowledge. Unfortunately, not all of it is useful; however, I believe this might help you. I have discovered two seasonal tendencies that could help you capture profits: one in the soybean market (which I describe in the next chapter) and the other in the wheat market.

Between 1983 and 1995, my trading business was located on the floor of the Grain Exchange where I met a very successful old-time trader. Other traders would ask this man's opinion, which was highly regarded because he was known as a successful trader. His response often was, "Listen to the 'Voice from the Tomb.'" Over the years, I befriended him and finally got up the nerve to ask him what he meant by this statement. He told me that the "Voice from the Tomb" (VFTT) was one of the secrets of his success, and the legend goes something like this:

Years ago, a millionaire grain trader lost his wife and dedicated his life to his three children. But as in many second generations of self-made people, the children were lazy and thought they would inherit all his money. As he aged, he began to look at his children as wasteful, and he believed they took him for granted. When he died, he left nothing to the children and instead gave all the money to charity. All he left them in his will were dates of when to buy and sell. The will stated that if they strictly followed his advice, they would have the fortune they had always expected to inherit.

Then my friend shared the VFTT dates for the wheat market:

- Sell March wheat on January 10
- Buy May wheat on February 22
- Sell July wheat on May 10
- Buy December wheat on July 1
- Sell December wheat on September 10
- Buy March wheat on November 28

He told me these dates worked for him 80% of the time (a remarkable percentage for a trading program), but he never shared exactly how he used them in his own trading. So I went back and studied the wheat charts.

I researched 35 years and found that the VFTT was historically profitable approximately 75% of the trades, based on the criteria I developed. The criteria was simple: I would buy or sell at the close of each date and risk 15¢ per bushel, or $750 per contract, to make 15¢, or $750 per contract. If a date fell on a Saturday, I would take the trade on the Friday close; if the date fell on a Sunday, I would use the Monday close. I started trading it with real money in 1999, and it worked nicely for eight years up until 2007. The actual results were as follows:

- 1999—Profitable five out of six trades
- 2000—Four of six
- 2001—Six of six (Chart 4.1)
- 2002—Four of six
- 2003—Four of six
- 2004—Three of six
- 2005—Five of six (Chart 4.2)
- 2006—Four of six

So during this eight-year period, I experienced 35 profits and only 13 losses. And in 2001, it was perfect—six trades and six profits (see Chart 4.1). The overall result was more than 70% profitable—a nice little program.

In 2005, it resulted in five profits and only one loss (see Chart 4.2).

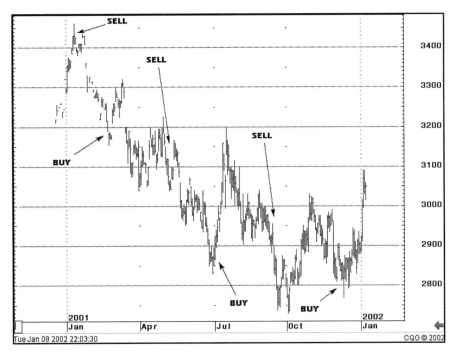

Chart 4.1   2001 wheat market

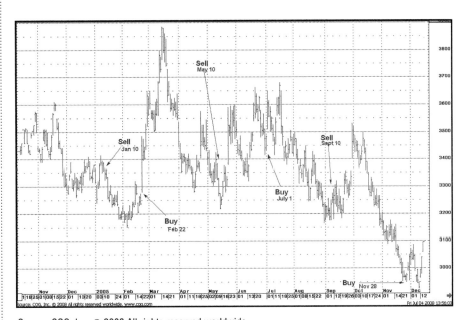

Chart 4.2   2005 wheat market

Since I began trading with real money, it had one break-even year, seven profitable years, and no losing years until 2007. In 2007, it self-destructed: The results were only two for six. What made that year worse was the first trade was a short sale that came out the day before a major crop report. The crop report was bullish, resulting in a sharp gap higher at the market open the day of the report and creating a 27¢ loss on our 15¢ stop. Now I needed two wins just to make up for that one loss, but, unfortunately, the next two trades were losers as well. This was also the first and only time since I had been trading the VFTT that it had three losing trades in a row. I told my clients that something had changed, something was not right. After eight years of a winning program, I retreated to the sidelines. As it turned out, two of the three remaining trades that year worked, but overall, this was the year the VFTT didn't work.

Then in the summer 2008, a client of mine who had been on the program for years and was still monitoring it asked if I had been watching the VFTT. He said that after we quit, it was working nicely again. During the last three trades of 2007 and the first four trades of 2008, it was five for seven—in other words, right back on track. So I took another look at the program that had been so good for so long, and this is what I discovered.

Remember the bad trade in January that took place right before a major crop report? If the signal had taken place one day later, at the close the day of the crop report, it would have worked. The May signal didn't work, and I gave up before the July signal, but that one worked like a champ. The September signal would not have worked, but if it had taken place one day later, it would have worked. And the November signal worked just fine. This told me that the basic seasonal tendencies still seemed to work, but something was off a day or two for certain signals. That something was the major *crop report* in both January and September, which skewed the program. And guess what? For decades, the crop report had come out on the 10th of the month. But due to date changes, the January report had come out a day later than the usual 10th date, as had the September report. I believe the VFTT works because it's based on normal seasonal tendencies for the wheat market. For example, the July buy signal takes place about the time the winter wheat harvest is approximately half over. Because many farmers sell their wheat crop right out of the fields at harvest time, the tendency is for prices to fall into the harvest period due to greater-than-normal supplies available to the marketplace at that time of year. The futures market anticipates the end of harvest and generally bottoms, and then starts to climb as the harvest period turns the corner and unwinds.

When a crop report comes out, traders react to it. A bullish report might be released during a normally weak seasonal period and might spike the market higher. However, in a normal year, the market tends to move along the normal seasonal path of least resistance after the news is out. Based on its stellar past, I believe it's time to revisit the VFTT program, but with one major modification. We need to look at the trading calendar to determine when the monthly crop report will be released. If a signal is due to take place the day before the report, wait a day and buy or sell at the close the day *of* the report. My theory is this: If the seasonal is bearish and the report is bullish, we will short the artificial spike and then let the bearish seasonal take over. If the report is bearish and we end up selling lower, the normal seasonal trend will bail us out anyway. This improvement would have turned a 2-and-4 year into a 4-and-2 year in 2007 and maintained the winning streak. As we go to press in 2008, the VFTT is solidly back on track; see Chart 4.3.

Source: CQG, Inc. © 2008 All rights reserved worldwide.

Chart 4.3   2008 wheat market

One last observation: Think of my 15¢ rule as an optimization rule. The trend often moves much farther, and you can make considerably more than the 15¢. Sometimes you need to take the 15¢ to 20¢, and other times you can make a lot more. Note the February 22 signal on the 2008 chart. The buy came at $10, and with zero risk on that signal, the market rallied above $12, or 200¢ ($10,000 per contract traded), *in just three trading sessions* before the first significant correction occurred. So you might want to wait and watch a bit when the profit target is met, and use a trailing stop. One method is to raise your stop to ensure a modest profit when the 15¢ number is reached, and try to maximize the trade.

Bottom line: I believe the VFTT will put the odds in your favor—just watch out for those crop reports.

Some traders believe that seasonals exist in many markets, but in my experience, I've observed them successfully only in the grain markets. "Voice" dates occur for corn as well. But my experience is that they're not as accurate as those for wheat, which is why I didn't include them here. However, I have discovered my own extremely reliable seasonal for the soybean market, which I present in the next chapter.

chapter 5

The Soy Secret
(Super Seasonal #2)

"Three may keep a secret, if two of them are dead."
—Benjamin Franklin

"The man who has no secrets from his wife either has no secrets or no wife."
—Gilbert Wells

In this chapter, I plan to share with you our second super seasonal called *the soy secret*.

The soy secret is simply this: *Soybeans exhibit a very strong tendency to form a seasonal price bottom during the month of October.* The large number of farmers who tend to sell their crop right out of the fields at harvest time to generate cash causes selling pressure and creates this bottoming tendency. Sometimes, particularly in high-priced years, this market behavior is more pronounced than others. *After the harvest selling pressure subsides, the soybean market tends to exhibit a post-harvest rally, offering a profitable trading opportunity.*

When I quantified the probabilities for a soybean price rise post-harvest, I discovered something quite exciting.

My database covers 40 years, from 1968 through 2008. In Table 5.1, I sorted this data not by year, but by the percentage gain the July (of the following year) soybean futures contract made from the October low price to the high for each year's July contract. (This is the last column.) The "Risk" column refers to the maximum price break (measured in cents per bushel) for that crop year *under* the October low price (post-October), and the "Gain" column measures (in cents per bushel) the highest price achieved after the October low was registered for the contract.

Table 5.1—July 2008 Soybeans (Sorted by Percentage Gain)

Year	Oct Low	Date of Oct Low	Post-Oct Low	Date of Low	Contract High	Date of High	Risk	Gain	% Gain
1981–82	**722**	**27 Oct**	**602**	**7 Jul**	**755**	**12 Oct**	**120**	**0**	**0.0%**
1990–91	**649**	**1 Oct**	**519**	**10 Jul**	**NA**	**9 Oct**	**130**	**0**	**0.0%**
1968–69	259	4 Oct	NA	NA	272	7 May	0	13	5.0%
1985–86	541	7 Oct	497	24 Nov	576	26 Dec	44	35	6.4%
1983–84	**828**	**27 Oct**	**720**	**14 Feb**	**899**	**25 May**	**108**	**72**	**8.6%**
1988–89	780	26 Oct	751	18 Nov	847	5 Jan	29	67	8.6%
2000–01	490	30 Oct	422	25 Apr	534	19 Dec	68	44	9.0%
1984–85	627	1 Oct	551	2 Jun	685	1 Nov	134	58	9.3%
1991–92	578	11 Oct	563	6 Jan	637	1 Jun	16	59	10.2%
2006–07	**585**	**10 Oct**	**565**	**28 Nov**	**650**	**4 Jan**	**20**	**65**	**11.1%**
1998–99	555	1 Oct	402	9 Jul	618	30 Nov	153	63	11.4%
2005–06	**585**	**10 Oct**	**565**	**28 Nov**	**650**	**4 Jan**	**20**	**75**	**12.8%**
1974–75	**803**	**28 Oct**	**490**	**3 Jun**	**NA**	**11 Nov**	**313**	**106**	**13.2%**
1979–80	713	29 Oct	595	2 Apr	816	17 Jul	118	103	14.4%
1971–72	319	5 Oct	313	13 Jan	366	18 Apr	6	47	14.7%
1994–95	564	7 Oct	559	1 Feb	649	17 Jul	5	85	15.1%
1989–90	579	16 Oct	578	29 Jan	672	1 May	1	93	16.1%
1970–71	300	1 Oct	290	26 Apr	351	19 Jul	10	50	16.7%
1993–94	628	8 Oct	NA	NA	733	23 May	0	105	16.7%

1997–98	643	1 Oct	607	9 Jun	753	11 Nov	36	110	17.1%
1999–00	497	29 Oct	465	13 Dec	583	3 May	32	86	17.3%
1982–83	570	26 Oct	NA	NA	673	11 Apr	0	103	18.1%
1969–70	250	1 Oct	NA	NA	299	29 Jun	0	49	19.6%
1980–81	856	3 Oct	673	29 Jun	1024	28 Nov	183	168	19.6%
1986–87	497	7 Oct	477	27 Feb	604	15 Jun	20	107	21.5%
2002–03	531	9 Oct	NA	NA	658	20 May	0	127	23.9%
1978–79	675	2 Oct	673	16 Nov	859	22 Jun	2	184	27.3%
1995–96	663	3 Oct	NA	NA	856	12 Jul	0	193	29.1%
2004–05	**535**	**18 Oct**	**506**	**4 Feb**	**696**	**16 Mar**	**29**	**161**	**30.1%**
2001–02	442	22 Oct	425	2 Jan	600	10 Jul	17	134	30.3%
1973–74	529	30 Oct	520	5 Nov	696	26 Feb	9	167	31.6%
1996–97	681	31 Oct	668	12 Nov	902	7 May	13	221	32.5%
1992–93	555	8 Oct	NA	NA	755	19 Jul	0	200	36.0%
1977–78	539	21 Oct	NA	NA	758	30 May	0	219	40.6%
1975–76	515	28 Oct	466	15 Dec	757	7 Jul	49	242	47.0%
2007–08	967	8 Oct	NA	NA	1660	3 Jul	0	693	66.1%
2003–04	639	6 Oct	NA	NA	1064	5 Apr	0	425	66.5%
1976–77	619	18 Oct	617	15 Nov	1064	22 Apr	2	445	71.9%
1987–88	546	20 Oct	540	3 Nov	1100	23 Jun	6	554	101.4%
1972–73	344	13 Oct	NA	NA	1290	5 Jun	0	946	275.0%

For example, the July 2008 soybeans neatly followed the pattern (Chart 5.1). The contract low was made on October 7th at $9.67 per bushel. A dramatic uptrend ensued, with an interim high (that went off this chart) in March at just below $16 per bushel. The actual contract high was reached during the delivery period in July at $16.60 per bushel. It would have been hard not to make some money this year using the soy secret.

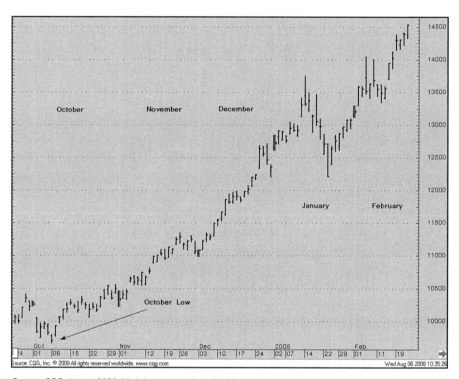

Source: CQG, Inc. © 2008 All rights reserved worldwide.

Chart 5.1   July 2008 soybeans (daily chart)

Let's analyze the data in Table 5.1 to develop a trading plan.

Looking at the last column first, we see only two years with zero gain— which means there were only two years when the month of October was the high-priced period for the July contract. For 38 of the 40 years, at least some price gain occurred above the October lows. However, trading is never as easy as buying in October and selling at a profit sometime later—we need to be realistic based on some risk-to-reward criteria. In the real trading world, I identified seven years (1974–75, 1981–82, 1983–84, 1990–91, 2004–05, 2005–06, and 2006–07) where I make the assumption that a trader who knew about this "October market secret" might not have profited because a measurable price drop from the October lows occurred before any big gains. For example, in 2006–07, even though the market eventually gained 11% from the October 2006 lows, I placed this year in the losing category because the market made a lower low in November. This November low was only 20¢ per bushel less than the October low and was followed by a big rally post-November, so it is certainly possible that a trader actually would have profited this year on the soy secret. However, to be conservative, I placed years such as this one in the losing category. Even if we include years such as this one in the red category (shown in bold in the table), we see an excellent chance to make a nice profit with minimal risk by buying in October for 33 of the 40 years (more than 80% of the time).

Remember that every year is different, and you have no guarantees or sure paths to profit. You might want to study the fundamentals of a particular year (acreage planted, carryover supplies, and projected demand) or look for a chart signal to confirm that the tendency is working this year. However, knowledge is power and understanding historical odds can only improve your odds for future success. And one last thought: How about we keep our "market secret" just between us?

chapter 6

The Significant News Indicator

"First the doctor told me the good news: I was going to have a disease named after me."
—Steve Martin

As long as markets have existed, savvy traders have paid attention to the market's reaction to significant (potentially market-moving) news. This was true in the days of the ticker tape and is still true in today's electronic age.

Significant news should, by definition, result in a significant market reaction. But it doesn't always happen, and many times the reaction is opposite of what's commonly expected. In this chapter, I present my "significant news indicator" (SNI). The SNI will help you trade the market's reaction to news. It's as much a trading philosophy as an indicator, but because we're able to apply specific rules to news reactions, the SNI can be as useful as any mathematical indicator.

To introduce the concept, consider this statement. What matters is not the news, but how the market reacts to the news. Certainly, the news sets the public perception, but you must be alert for divergences between the news and market action. It's *expectation versus reality*. Look for the divergence between what's happening and what people think is supposed to happen. When the big turn comes, the general public will always be looking the wrong way.

Remember that losing January Voice from the Tomb (VFTT) short sale, when the market gapped higher after a bullish crop report? The news was bullish, and although the market reacted to it initially, the underlying fundamentals were bearish, and the market ultimately could not hold on to the gains the news created. When the wheat market couldn't hold the initial gains, the market was telling a trader to listen to it and not to the news; it was saying that the seasonal tendency of the VFTT was ultimately correct, particularly when wheat futures fell below the price posted before the release of the "bullish" news.

Six News Rules

1. If bad news is announced and the market starts to sell off in large volume, it's a good bet that the market's going lower.

2. If the market fails to react to good news, it probably already has been discounted in the price.

3. Moves of importance invariably tend to begin before any news justifies the initial price move. When the move is underway, the emerging fundamentals will slowly come to light. *A big rally (decline) on no news is usually very bullish (bearish).*

4. It is generally not a good practice to buy after very bullish news or sell after an extremely bearish report, because both good and bad news can already be discounted in the price.

5. Always consider whether the trend is down or up when the news is made known because a well-established trend will generally continue regardless of the news. I remember getting caught in the emotion of a very bullish corn report in January 1994. Looking back, this news was the very top. An opposite (very bearish) report the following year turned out to be the springboard for one of the biggest corn bull markets in history and led me to develop the SNI.

6. When unexpected news occurs (news that the market has not had time to prepare for) and the market opens in a wide range or "gaps" lower or higher, sell out your longs or cover your shorts and wait. Watch the market for 30 minutes to an hour. If the market opened sharply lower with heavy selling and was not able to trade much lower than that, it's into support, and you can buy it with a tight risk point. Watch the market closely at this point and note the tone of the rally. If it's small and the market is able to again fall under the levels made when the bad news came out (or rise above the levels made when the good news came out), it's safe to assume the market is going lower (higher).

I remember the big bull coffee move of 1994. One day the market was trading in the mid-80¢ level. I was long. Unexpected news hit the wires about the surprise government release of massive Brazilian stockpiles of coffee. These stocks were supposed to be held in reserve and off the market, but Brazil needed foreign exchange at the time and changed its policy. The market gapped lower at the open and proceeded to trade down 400 points, stopping me out in the process. It remained weak for a day or so, but as soon as the market was able to cross above the mid-80¢ level again (the price registered before the unexpected bad news hit), it basically went straight up. This was the time to reenter. It was up to about $1.40 *before* the first freeze hit. The full move wasn't over until coffee prices hit close to $2.75, and the monster bull run began when the market, on *no* news, crossed the level made before the release of the bad news.

In summer 1999, the British Central Bank announced it was going to auction off half of its gold reserves, calling gold a "barbaric relic." The price was about $250 per ounce, and although this news was bearish (flooding an already weak market with massive additional supply), this was *the* absolute bottom.

The bearish crop report of 1995 led to me to develop the SNI (although I did not formally put a name to it until this book). We were moving from Minnesota to Lake Tahoe and driving along Interstate 80 on the day of the report—August 11, 1995. I had a large long position in the December corn for clients and myself. At that time, the crop was looking good and nobody knew the weather would turn unfavorable late that summer, creating a short crop. I must have had my reasons for being long, but my hopes were dashed when the crop report was released before the market open that day. I remember calling my assistant from the road when he told me "limit down." The crop report was so bearish in reporting an increased size of the upcoming crop that the early calls were for the market to open down the (then) 10¢–per-bushel limit. And not only limit down, but the early banter was that the market would open limit down and "lock," meaning I could get stuck in my position with only offers to sell limit down and no bids at that price. It made me uncomfortable as I sweated out the hour and a half before the market's open, trying to decide how I'd work out of this mess from the road. I asked my assistant to call me right before the market opened and give me a blow by blow.

The market did open sharply lower—7¢ lower, to be exact—but not limit down, to our surprise. The market gave me, and anyone else who was long, a chance to get out and save our skins before a limit-down move. But instead of trading lower from the 7¢-lower open, my assistant told me corn was beginning to trade up from the 7¢-lower open. It felt as if a cloud were lifted, and my nervousness disappeared. I told him to place a stop on our entire position just below the opening price of 270 (see Chart 6.1).

Source: CQG, Inc. © 2008 All rights reserved worldwide.

Chart 6.1   December 1995 corn

I continually checked in that day, but the stop was never hit. When the market was trading higher for the day, I instinctively knew I was safe. That 270 low registered because of the bearish news was a major low that was never challenged again the rest of that year. It actually turned out to be a significant low that held up for years, and it was the springboard for one of the biggest bull moves in history. By the next year, due to crop problems in the United States and globally (China turned from the largest corn exporter in Asia into an importer), corn prices had doubled.

The SNI is a fairly simple, but powerful, concept: *The SNI is the price at which a market is trading just before the release of a significant market news event.* The news is generally a preplanned event; however, it can also be unexpected.

SNI Rules

Here's how to successfully use the SNI in your trading:

1. If the news is considered bullish, the SNI is your major support number and, if acting properly, the market *should* remain above it. If the market is acting properly after a bullish event, you can enter a long position with a stop just below the SNI.

2. After a bullish news event, a move below the SNI generates an automatic sell signal, and you can immediately enter a short sale with a tight stop just above the SNI.

3. If the news is considered bearish, the SNI is your major resistance number and the market *should* remain below it if acting properly. If the market is acting properly after a bearish event, you can enter a short position with a stop just above the SNI.

4. After a bearish news event, a move above the SNI generates an automatic buy signal, and you can immediately enter a long position with a tight stop just below the SNI.

When the SNI is crossed, it tells a trader when to enter and where to place a protective stop. However, it doesn't tell a trader when to exit a profitable position. (Other technical indicators or a trailing stop should be used for that.)

It's important to know what the market is expecting before the release of the news event so that you can accurately judge whether the market is acting properly. For example, if a crop report is to be released and the market is expecting an increase in soybean acreage of 2 million acres, an increase of 1 million is bullish news. You would need to know the average "guesstimate" or expectation before the release to accurately evaluate the report and the market's reaction to it.

I've instinctively used the SNI after every crop report for many years. I simply evaluate the market's reaction versus expectation.

For example, the October 2006 crop report was considered bullish for corn. The market was anticipating a record-large (bearish) corn crop estimate of more than 11 billion bushels on the USDA report; however, the crop size was reduced by 2% and was well under this figure. The market closed the day before the report at 284 (this was the SNI) and opened limit up at 304 the day the report was released (see Chart 6.2).

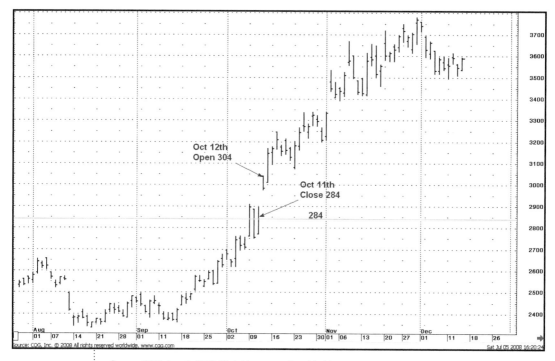

Chart 6.2   December 2006 corn

The market was not able to remain limit up that day and gave ample opportunity to enter a new long position, based on our first rule. The sell stop should
have been placed at just under 284, the closing price before the report's release.
For the remainder of that year, countless opportunities arose for traders to take
a decent profit entering *after* the bullish news was well known to the marketplace.

In contrast, that same report was considered very bearish for soybeans. The
market was looking for an unchanged soybean crop estimate; however, the
USDA report indicated the crop size was more than 3 billion bushels for the first
time ever. This was up 3% from the September report and was record large.

The January 2007 soybean futures closed the day before the report's release
at 577; however, the market opened higher at 588 after the "bearish" number.
The SNI was therefore 577, and a higher open was an immediate and automatic
buy signal according to our fourth rule, with an initial sell stop just below 577
(see Chart 6.3). The market continued to climb until the end of November. Even
though the number was considered "bearish," the Chinese turned out to be
major buyers of soybeans for the remainder of the year, pushing prices much

higher (although a trader could not have known that at the time of the report). However, the market certainly knew this, leaving countless footprints in the sand. Take another look at Chart 6.3. On the day of the "bearish" report, you'll also see a beautiful breakout from a consolidation. The news didn't matter as much as how the market reacted to this news.

Chart 6.3 January 2007 soybeans

The SNI works not only with crop reports, but also with financial reports and other news events, both expected and surprise.

Every Wednesday, the oil inventory report is released at 10:30 AM EST. This number typically moves the oil market, sometimes sharply. This is an example of a typical reaction to a bullish supply number: On this report day the first week in June, just before the release of the number, the nearby oil futures were trading at 12230. The market was looking for a slight drawdown in weekly oil stocks, but the actual number was a 5 million barrel drawdown—bullish. The market immediately traded higher and, within a minute, was trading above 12300 (see Chart 6.4). The market exhibited a bullish reaction to the news and was acting properly.

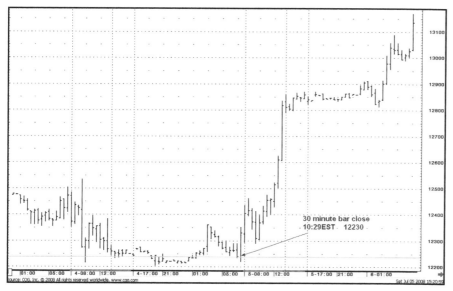

30 minute bar close
10:29EST 12230

Chart 6.4   June 5, 2008, bullish inventory report

After the market moved higher fast, many traders would have shied away, believing the news was already out and discounted. However, this was an opportunity based on our first rule. The chart looked good, the market was acting correctly, and you could enter a long position with a stop just below the 12230 SNI, the price just before the release of the news. The reason? If the market is any good, it shouldn't be able to trade below the point just before the release of the bullish news. Subsequently, the market ran above 12400, corrected, made a higher low at approximately 12300 (at which time the stop could be raised to just below this higher low), and a trailing stop could have be used. During the following 48 hours, this particular move ran up to 13900— more than $13 or $13,000 per contract—before the first significant correction took place.

Two weeks later, another "bullish" inventory report was released with a higher-than-anticipated drawdown. Just before the release, the market was trading at 13700. This number should have been noted as the SNI. The market immediately traded higher (acted properly), up to 13836. However, within an hour after the number was released, the market reversed and quickly moved below the 13700 SNI (see Chart 6.5). Unlike two weeks earlier, it was able to trade below the point before the release of the bullish news. This is bearish action according to our second rule. A trader could have gone short on a stop just below this 13700 number and, if filled, place a buy stop just above.

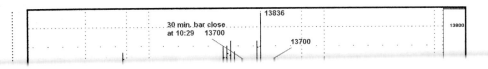

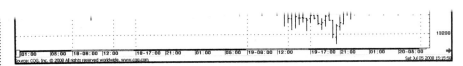

Chart 6.5   June 18, 2008, bullish inventory report

Within the following 24 hours, the opportunity arose to make up to $5,000-per-contract profit on the short side with effectively zero risk after entry. Note that the SNI doesn't tell you when to exit a profitable position. It signals an entry point. You can make the stop close to your entry point, but an alternative method is required to signal your exit. You can judiciously utilize a trailing stop. In this example, we saw a reversal bar at the lows with a mini H&S bottoming pattern that signaled the bottom.

The following week, the number was bearish, with a larger-than-expected stock build. Just before the release of the number, the oil market was trading at 13570 (see Chart 6.6).

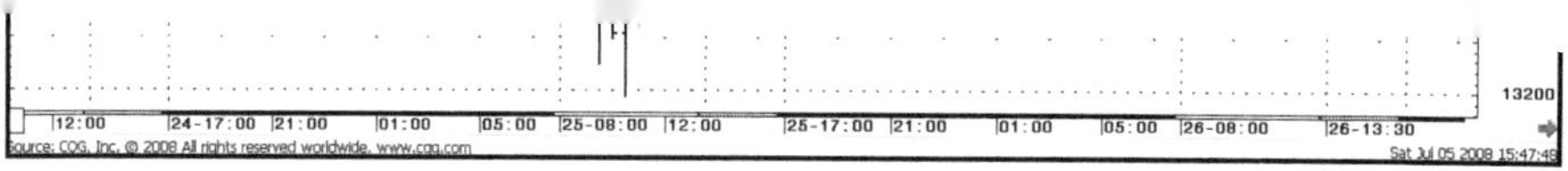

13200

Chart 6.6   June 25, 2008, bearish inventory report

After the release of the numbers, the market was initially acting properly—bearishly—and a nimble trader could have gone short by utilizing a trailing stop. The market subsequently bottomed below 13200. But the following day, it was able to trade above the "bearish" number, and this was a bullish sign. Hopefully, if short, a profit was "locked in" via the use of a trailing stop. However, if still short, the minute the market crossed above the 13570 level, all shorts should be immediately covered and new longs could be entered with a tight stop. The market is now trading above the level of the bearish news, and this is a bullish development according to our fourth rule. Even though this occurred a day later, it was still within a fairly short time period. This is why it's important to note the price level just before the release of significant news—the SNI. SNIs are important numbers and often will act as major support or resistance for days—even weeks—into the future.

This works equally well for financial news events. For example, in July 2008, it was anticipated that the European Central Bank would raise rates by a quarter-point, but it actually raised rates by a half-point. Just before the announcement, the euro was trading at 15815. Just after the announcement, it acted properly by trading higher, reaching 15853 within an hour. However, that same day, the market crossed below the 15815 level, the price just before the announcement. A sell stop could have been used at just below this number (for example 15810), based on our second rule. In what turned out to be a zero-risk trade, the market collapsed 200 points, or $2,500 per contract, and traded in short order (see Chart 6.7).

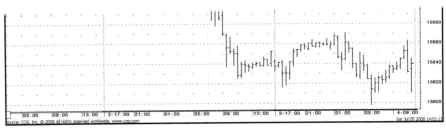

Chart 6.7   July 3, 2008, euro 30-minute chart

I could fill a book with examples similar to these; they occur almost every day. When you know an important report (a crop report, an unemployment report, a Fed interest rate announcement, an inventory report, or a stock earnings report) will be released, note where the market is trading just before the release. This level will be your SNI, and you can use it to successfully trade against—usually setting up trading opportunities with high potential reward in relation to the risk. It's all based on the simple premise that is key to successful trading: What matters is not the news, but how the market reacts to the news.

chapter 7

"Perfect numbers, like perfect men, are very rare."
—Rene Descartes

In golf, "par" denotes an ideal score for the best golfers, but the generally accepted definition of par is merely "average or ordinary." Therefore, "above par" has come to mean an above-average or extraordinary event.

In the financial markets, trading "above par"—above the psychologically significant number of 100—is considered an important market milestone. If the price of a bond is trading above 100 (for example, at 106), it's trading "above par" and at a "premium." This is a sign of strength. If the same bond falls and subsequently trades down to 94, it would be trading at a "discount" or "under par."

Although the number 100 should have no greater significance than any other integer, in the real world, I've discovered that crossing above 100—the breaking of par—is quite significant from a trading standpoint. For example, it was a global news event when our dodo pit trader overpaid for his $100 oil contract.

You can apply this same rule to any big round number, such as 500 or 900; however, those beginning with a 1 and ending in two or more zeros (100, 1,000, and 10,000) are considered the patriarchs.

The loudest cheers ever to ring out from the floor of the New York Stock Exchange resounded on November 14, 1972, when the Dow Jones Industrial Average crossed the 1,000 mark for the first time. This was the most important psychological barrier for the Dow ever. For the previous six years, it had tried

On April 1, 2004, the price of one share of the Chicago Mercantile Exchange (CME) first crossed 100, closing that session at $100.50 per share (Chart 7.1). If at that time you believed this all-time high price was "too high" and you waited for a return to double digits to be a buyer, you'd still be waiting. After the first cross of 100, CME quickly ran to 130 and then 148 before the first meaningful correction. It subsequently has traded as high as 700, and back down to 400, but it has never again traded below par.

Source: CQG, Inc. © 2008 All rights reserved worldwide.

Chart 7.1   2003–2004 Chicago Mercantile Exchange

This magical rule of breaking par and continuing upward is one that I've long observed and traded successfully for many years, but it's not my discovery. I first paid attention to this concept after reading *Reminiscences of a Stock Operator*,

100 on the tape when the ticker was only printing 98. So I said to myself, "I can't wait until it gets through 100. I have to get it now. It is as good as gone through par." ...I put in an order to buy 500 shares of Bethlehem Steel. The market was then 98. I got 500 shares at 98 to 99. After that she shot right up and closed that night at 115. I bought 500 shares more. The next day Bethlehem Steel was at 145 and I had my stake. But I earned it. Those six weeks of waiting for the right moment were the most strenuous and wearing six weeks I ever put in.

This rule holds equally true for commodities.

When sugar first crossed above 100 on the monthly chart (10¢ per pound equals 1000 on the tape) in August 2005, it didn't stop there. It quickly ran above 1100, then above 1200, and then above every XX00 until the move was finally over with the February 2006 peak at a price of 1973 (Chart 7.2).

Chart 7.2   2005 monthly sugar

A "Par" Case Study

In late 2007, the soybean market was in a bull trend. The carryover supplies for 2008 were projected to be very tight, and I was watching the July–November 2008 soybean spread for a possible cross above 100.

July soybeans represent the current crop (the crop that was harvested the previous autumn), and November soybeans represent the "new" crop (the crop that will be harvested the following year). Soybeans are planted in the spring and harvested in the fall. When trading futures, we are certainly dealing with the unknown—too an extent—and we knew very little in late 2007 about the November 2008 beans because this contract represented a crop that was not planted yet. Preliminary estimates were available on the acreage farmers would plant in the spring, but these planting intentions would certainly change based on the price of soybeans versus competing crops. We knew nothing about weather, potential yields, demand, and so on. Anyone buying or shorting November beans was certainly betting on the unknown. We knew more about the "old" July crop because this crop was already harvested. The old crop price had been fluctuating, and would continue to fluctuate, based on demand (for exports, biofuels, livestock feed, and the hundreds of other soy uses) plus differing opinions and future changes in the official supply numbers. July comes near the end of the crop year, and the ultimate price of July soybeans in July is dependent on ending-crop-year supplies being tight or plentiful at this time before the new crop becoming available. This spread historically is volatile

new and potentially profitable trading opportunity. The question was, how to play it? As you read this case study, remember that it is pertinent to all markets, not just the July–November soybean spread. I want to give you a feel for how I approach a potential trade, and this is designed to provide you with a template for analyzing and hopefully successfully trading any market that crosses par.

The first step was background analysis, to find and then analyze what I call analog years of this spread. Analog years always have one characteristic in common. For example, we can analyze all drought years for the soybean market—in this case, a spread break above 100—but remember that no two markets act identically.

I knew that this spread had been above par in the past, but not very often. It is a highly unusual event for the July contract to be trading $1 per bushel above the November contract. The "normal" spread is the cost of carry—what it costs to hold soybeans for about five months (mostly the cost of money and storage)—and this number (depending on the prevailing interest rate and the raw bean price) has historically been about 5¢–10¢ per bushel per month. For the spread to be trading at a $1 difference or higher means something quite unusual is taking place beyond the normal supply-and-demand balance between two consecutive crop years.

Using CQG historical data, I could find only six previous years when the July contract traded at or above 100 more than the following November contract: 1973, 1984, 1989, 1994, 1997, and 2004.

I then examined these analog years to see how the spread acted on a break of 100. For example, look at Chart 7.3 of the July–November 2004 spread.

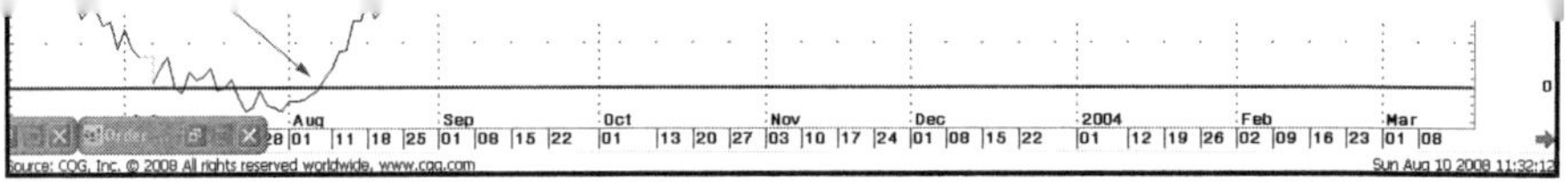

Chart 7.3 July–November 2004 soybean spread

After the spread crossed 100 in this year, it never looked back. If you entered the spread on the first cross of 100 (or even on the first close above 100) and risked to a close below, you would never have been in trouble. The minimum profit objective of a 15%–30% move (or 115 to 130), as outlined in the "profit objective zone" on Chart 7.4, was easily attained. In fact, the spread traded above 200 this year.

Now that we were armed with this historical knowledge, we were ready to trade the 2007 spread because we knew what to look for when it was trading properly. This year, the spread first broke and closed above 100 on November 29, with the close at a 103 premium for the July contract—a buy signal (see Chart 7.4). However, the next day, it broke and closed under par at 96, indicating that this was a false signal. The proper action at this time was to take the loss of approximately 4¢–7¢, depending on our entry point.

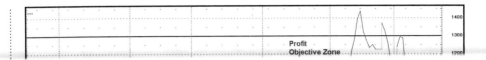

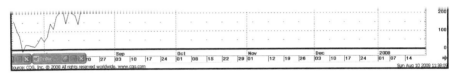

Chart 7.4   July–November 2008 soybean spread

The spread remained below par until December 10, when it once again crossed and closed above—a new buy signal. The correct play was to reenter, and this time the profit objective zone was quickly and easily reached and, ultimately, exceeded. However, note that the profit should have been locked in at the first sign of a trend reversal. (Tip: You can also use a moving average line to help identify trend reversals on spreads.) If it weren't turned into real cash, the profit eventually evaporated because the spread collapsed after it crossed back under 100 in January. Actually, this theory works both ways. You can play a cross under 100 just as effectively as a cross above. Just reverse the rules and always pay attention to your money management.

Livermore's timeless observation that breaking par often results in a quick and significant follow-through is a powerful concept. Don't forget it, and plan to revisit it.

chapter 8

"When in doubt, predict that the present trend will continue."
—Anonymous

"History doesn't repeat itself, but it does rhyme."
—Mark Twain

The title of this chapter might rhyme and sound clever, but don't underestimate it. When talking about successful trading, these words are some of the most profound around.

A successful trader once told me, "If you can correctly determine the trend of a market, you *will* make money." Although this might sound like a simple concept, it's not easy to accomplish in the real world.

The reason you'll make money when you correctly identify the trend is that the odds favor your position, showing a profit in short order. Even if your timing is initially off, if you have correctly identified the major trend, many times the trend will bail you out. On the other hand, when you attempt to pick tops or bottoms, you must be extremely nimble in booking any available profits because they'll be fleeting—when the trend reasserts itself, those contra-trend profits will quickly evaporate.

Just as it's much easier to swim with the current than against it, and easier to walk with the wind than against it, it's generally much easier to trade with the trend than against it. The trick is how to determine the prevailing trend—and determine it early enough to reap the benefit.

market trend determination and touch on how to potentially stay out of trouble. I use the "Keep It Simple, Stupid" (KISS) method here because simple is often better (at least, for my simple mind). The concepts presented here will be familiar to many of you, but bear with me because this dovetails into Chapter 9, "The Natural Number Method," where I introduce a new, simple, yet powerful, commodity-trading system that forms the heart of this book.

On the soybean chart shown in Chart 8.1, the trend is up. You can't dispute this fact because the soybeans registered a new contract high price on the last date. There's a statistical means of saying what we know to be true here. Statistics are most useful when we are unsure of the trend, and the statistic we use here is the 50-day weighted moving average (WMA). (If you are unfamiliar with how moving averages work or with the differences between the moving averages types, skip to the moving averages primer in the Appendix, "A Moving Average Primer, an Open Interest Primer, and the Advanced Open Interest Course.")

I've drawn the 50-period (50-day, in this case, because it's a daily chart) weighted moving average on Chart 8.1. In KISS terms, the beans are in an uptrend because the market is trading *above* its 50-day WMA.

What if we're not long the beans from an earlier (lower) price and we'd like to be—should we buy them here? You can eyeball it and see that the market is trading well above its 50-day WMA (11.5% is significantly above). Therefore, if we risk to a move below the 50-day WMA (risking to a downtrend), we're assuming a significant dollar risk. Certainly, I wouldn't want to go short in this market, either—that would be top picking. Top picking would have been unprofitable at any prior period on this chart—extremely unprofitable if attempted weeks earlier. How would we have known that any one of the previous days (let alone the most recent day) was the top? The trend is up and soybeans could certainly move higher; however, buying late in the trend makes a purchase riskier from a risk-to-reward standpoint. Therefore, there are better trades out there, at least until a correction when the risk would be more

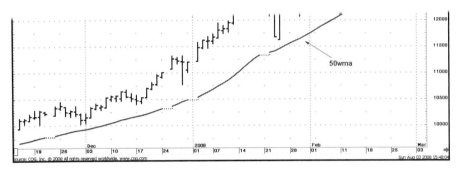

Source: CQG, Inc. © 2008 All rights reserved worldwide.

Chart 8.1   November soybeans (December–February)

What if you had bought the beans when they had *last* crossed above the 50-day WMA? The last break above the line actually occurred months before this chart began—the previous October, at 914—*and the market had not been able to close under the 50-dayWMA since that date.* A trader would be up more than $5 per bushel at the end of this chart (late February). That's more than $25,000 per contract, and the risk at the first cross was minimal. If you had bought beans on that first cross above during the previous October, and you had the discipline and patience to still be holding in February, your dilemma now would be when to take your massive profit—the best kind of dilemma to have.

Now let's turn our attention to this natural gas chart (see Chart 8.2), a market in a confirmed downtrend. We know this natural gas is in a downtrend because it is close to new lows and trading below the 50-day line. This chart is a mirror image of the soybean chart.

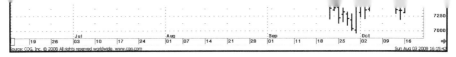

Chart 8.2   December natural gas

If we are bearish and not yet short, should we consider shorting natural gas here? It's "cheap," just slightly (about 3%) below its 50-day WMA, so the risk in shorting is reasonable (assuming we plan to risk just above the moving average line). What if we had sold on the first break of the 50-day WMA on August 30, just below 1025? If a trader had shorted just one contract on that close, he or she would be up $25,000 per contract by the end of the chart (a period of less than two months) and again with minimal risk. Actually, the 50-day WMA helped me here because I was bullish at the end of August, and the close under the 50-day WMA was one of the indicators that kept me out of big trouble. By selling out on the first break under, I took a small loss on that trade—but, more important, this prevented a large loss. Should I have gone short on the cross day? Sure, in the ideal world, I would have had a position up nearly $25,000 per contract. In the real world, it's hard to go against your fundamental bias. Once again, the 50-day WMA was much smarter than I was— "the market is always right." I cannot emphasize this enough: The trend is your friend, and don't fight the trend.

Don't get me wrong. I'm not saying this is foolproof, and false signals will certainly happen. For example, take a look at the sugar chart in Chart 8.3. It's a well-defined downtrend, but you can see the glaringly false buy signal on that two-day temporary spike above the average in early March.

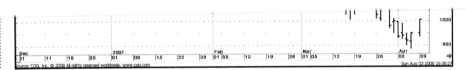

Chart 8.3   July sugar

I'm saying that this simple indicator—the moving average—many times will keep you out of trouble and improve your odds of positioning on the right side of the trend.

One of the keys to success is to look for markets that are close to their moving average. This alerts us to potential changes in trend (when the line is crossed) or a confirmation that the trend is still intact (if it's not crossed or bounces off the line). For example, the advantage of taking a trade just as the 50-day WMA is crossed is that you can reduce the risk on the trade. If you risk to a close on the other side of the line, your risk per trade is comparatively much lower than taking a trade well above or below the line. And you certainly will experience times when your risk will be very low, with a huge potential reward.

Another key to success in markets (and life in general) is to just go with the flow—don't fight the trend. Keep this concept in the forefront of your mind as we now plow ahead to a simple yet powerful commodity-trading system.

chapter 9

"It's tough to make predictions, especially about the future."
—Yogi Berra

Jesse Livermore's theory on breaking par works—I've seen it in action many times. But if we waited for that 100 number to place a trade, we wouldn't make that many trades. That 100 number is rare, and plenty of markets have exceeded it without ever dropping back under it again. It's highly doubtful that gasoline will ever again sell for $1 per gallon or gold for $100 an ounce. Still, Livermore's theorem got me thinking. Is breaking through round numbers significant, and if 100 represents a significant barrier, then how about 200 or 300?

Markets tend to behave differently at the significant break points—numbers that end in zero. I call these *natural numbers*, and numbers that end in two or more zeros I call *master natural numbers*. Livermore's theorem got me thinking about using natural numbers in conjunction with trend identifiers to design a methodology to profit in today's electronic marketplace. More about this shortly, but first, let's again discuss identifying trends.

A basic tenet of this book is that, with computers and the Internet, markets move faster than ever before. For example, the corn market has been one of the tamer commodities for decades, moving an average of 20¢–30¢ per bushel in a month's time—the equivalent of $1,000–$1,500 per contract traded. However, a well-capitalized account because the market plummeted as low as 513 on March 24. If you took a vacation, the margin clerk would have probably sold you out during that sharp break sometime between March 13 and March 24 when the market collapsed from 590 all the way down to the lows seven trading days later.

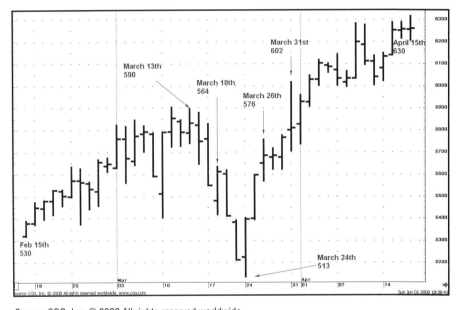

Chart 9.1   December corn (daily chart for February–April 2008)

If you were a bull and a bottom picker, and were fortunate enough to have bought the exact bottom at 513 on March 24, you were never in trouble. The truth is, catching the exact bottom is just about impossible. And as the old

period to provide more detail than the daily chart can provide. Chart 9.2 shows the 30-minute chart for that six-day period. (Each vertical bar now represents 30 minutes of trading versus one full day per bar in the daily chart.) Later I will explain why we picked the 30-minute chart over a faster or slower interval, but for now, just take this in.

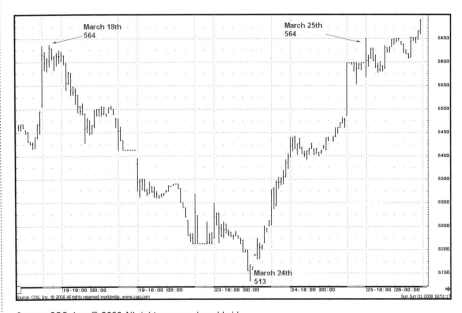

Source: CQG, Inc. © 2008 All rights reserved worldwide.

Chart 9.2   December corn (30-minute chart for March 18–25)

So we've come full circle back to the $64 question: what's the most important information we need to know to profit in a particular market scenario? I believe that it's the *trend* of the market. Livermore once said something to this effect: "When trading, if you can correctly determine the trend of a market, you *will* make money." This makes sense because if you're correct on the trend, you can successfully position yourself on the right side of the market. Even if your timing is initially off but you have identified the major trend correctly, the trend will often bail you out. But how can we determine what the market trend is at any point in time and when the trend has changed? By eyeballing the previous chart, you could easily determine that the trend was down March 18–24 and then sharply up into the 25th (and we also know this from viewing the daily chart into mid-April). Hindsight is always 20/20, but in the thick of the battle, it's not easy to determine the major underlying trend. This period no doubt would have wrecked havoc with a fundamental trader because these moves didn't appear to coincide with the "news." However, one of the tenets of technical analysis suggests that *if the markets appear irrational, you are missing something important, and the more irrational the trend appears, the more likely it's real*. The primary question remains, at any single point in time: How would you really have known what the trend is or when it had exhausted itself?

When using a moving average to analyze a market's trend, I recommend basing the calculations on the *closes* and using either *exponential* or *weighted* averages. In my experience, although the simple moving average will generate similar signals, I've found either the weighted moving average (WMA) or the smoothed exponential moving average (EMA) to be slightly better. The real conundrum is which length to use. Shorter-term averages are more sensitive.

With a more sensitive average, the good news is that your average loss will be smaller, but the bad news is that the "whipsaw factor" increases geometrically. A long string of small losses is no better than a small string of large losses, and

Chart 9.3 March 18–25 corn (30-minute with 180 period WMA)

By using a longer-term moving average (in this case, a 180-period average) superimposed on a shorter-term chart (in this case, a 30-minute chart), we increase our odds of being on the right side of the prevailing trend. However, if we bought every time a market traded above a moving average and sold every time it traded back below, we would be in and out of the market too often during choppy periods, leading to whipsaw activity.

is a *natural number.* Therefore, 300 is a master natural number, 320 is a natural number, and 322 or 323 are common numbers.

Humans generally view natural numbers as significant. If your car odometer is rolling over to 10,000 or 100,000, don't you want to see this? If you have people in the car and the odometer hits 49,999, you will probably make an announcement to your passengers so that everyone can see the rollover to 50,000, right? Businesses and individuals go to extra effort to get a phone number such as 456-7000 or a post office box number such as 3400 because round numbers are easier to remember. Recall how people around the globe celebrated the new millennium at the beginning of the year 2000? Even though the event wouldn't really occur until the end of that year (the beginning of 2001), 2000 was a really big deal—and I don't remember New Year's 2001 as having the same pizazz.

In the universe of numbers, natural numbers are rarer than their common brothers and sisters and, therefore, hold a special significance to people. People make markets, and any student of the markets has probably observed that volumes generally increase at the natural numbers. I wondered if natural numbers would also act as significant support or resistance points.

Livermore first pointed me in this direction. After extensive testing, I determined that natural numbers possessed statistically greater odds of being important support and resistance levels than random numbers. I then used this information to develop the trading methodology that I will share with you shortly, but consider this simple explanation of what lies ahead. Suppose gold broke above a significant moving average at the price of $897. Should we be a buyer at the market or would it be prudent to wait for the market to move to the next natural number (in this case, the master natural number $900) to be a buyer? In an uptrend, the downside of waiting would be to forfeit $3 of potential profit. The upside of waiting could be fewer whipsaws. What if the market broke under a significant moving average at $897? The closest lower

identify them, it's even more difficult to turn them into realized profits. Successful trading is more than identifying opportunities; it requires knowledge, discipline, and patience. Keep all this in mind as we move on to this new breakthrough strategy for capturing market profits.

In the following pages, I introduce you to a trading method that I designed and use myself that has never been in print previously. It's a dynamic trading strategy that you can apply across a wide variety of markets. It's designed to capture profits in the electronic commodity markets and is based on the philosophy that natural numbers represent significant price points.

Although I've personally found this trading methodology useful, please do *not* blindly follow it as outlined. Before trading real money, familiarize yourself with the concepts presented here and then paper-test them on any market of your choosing. Only when you've convinced yourself that what's presented here is useful and you're risking money that you can afford to lose should you consider applying it. And one more thing: Whether you use my program, you should be trading real money only if the following true disclaimer doesn't scare you away.

be liquidated at a loss, and you will be liable for any resulting deficit in your account. Under certain market conditions, you might find it difficult or impossible to liquidate a position. This can occur, for example, when the market makes a "limit move." Placing contingent orders, such as a "stop-loss" or "stop-limit" order, will not necessarily limit your losses to the intended amount.

There is no guarantee that the concepts presented in this book will generate profits or avoid losses.

Past results are not necessarily indicative of future results.

Phew, now that we got that out of the way, let's get to it. But first a few words about what this is not: This is not an "investment" strategy. It is not for "buy and holders." It is designed for commodity-futures traders who understand the risks and rewards associated with a leveraged vehicle. It is designed for above-average returns but has the associated above-average risks. You can universally apply specific rules for the system over many markets; however, specific markets possess variables based on the prevailing market tone. I am *not* teaching you how to trade. Learning to trade successfully requires more than one book. Instead, I provide you with a method that should help you. I give you a step-by-step outline for how to use and apply it. I give you no guarantees here. Regardless of how or what you trade, always remember that we are dealing with the unknown, and nothing is foolproof. With that said, I believe what is presented here can be a valuable technical tool that will help you to determine and successfully ride the prevailing trend. And as Livermore told us, "When trading, if you can correctly determine the trend of a market, you *will* make money."

The Natural Number Method (N#M)

that this is a dynamic number—the natural number method using the 180-period WMA is useful over a diversified portfolio of uncorrelated markets. N#M involves using a longer-term average over a shorter-term time frame to determine the trend. Other similar periods work just as well, but for this methodology I've found that less than 100 is too sensitive and more than 200 lags too much. The 180-period WMA is the constant; the variable is the optimal time period to use for a particular market and for varying market conditions.

Next, use the 180-period WMA to determine the major trend.

N#M Rules: Buy Signal

Entering a new trade from the long side requires three steps:

1. The setup

2. The confirmation

3. The buy signal

The Setup On the short-term chart, a bar (for example, the 15-minute chart generates one bar every 15 minutes) must *close above* the average. This forms the *setup bar* and creates the setup. (Note that merely *trading* above the 180-period WMA *does not* qualify as a setup because the market could subsequently trade back under the 180-period WMA line before the bar's close. A true setup is created only on a *close* above the line.)

The Confirmation After the setup is created, the market must subsequently exceed the high price of the setup bar. The confirmation occurs immediately if the market trades above the high price of the setup bar.

buy signal is canceled, and the process begins again. In this case, we wait for a new setup, confirmation, and buy (or sell) signal, with trade entry at the closest natural number. However, in this example, we will automatically be stopped in a new long position if the market trades up to 12800. After being stopped in a new buy, the sell stop on this new long position will initially be placed at the closest lower natural number (in the case of oil, the next lower master natural number of 12700). After a new trade is executed, the stop will be trailed—for a buy, raised one natural number every time a new higher natural number is exceeded until the trend turns and the market takes us out. When we're out, we wait for the next set up, confirmation, and signal. You might be totally confused at this point; however, this will all become clearer as we move forward.

Although I'm sure most of you know how to read a simple bar chart, look at the example in Chart 9.4 that uses a 15-minute bar chart for crude oil. First note the "no setup" bar on the left. This bar traded above the moving average line but closed below it (the horizontal "flag" to the right of each bar is the bar close), so it was not a setup. The setup occurred on the first close above the 180-period WMA at 12685. The high of this setup bar was 12697, and this number was exceeded on the subsequent bar in the move above 12697 (the confirmation). The next-closest natural number was 12700. After the setup bar closed and confirmed, a trader could immediately place a buy stop at the 12700 master natural number because he or she could observe the confirmation, and the buy signal would likely occur in short order. After the buy signal was entered (a new long at 12700), the trader would place a sell stop at the next master natural number lower (in this case, 12600). The risk on this trade was predetermined at 100 points, or $1,000 per contract (plus any slippage and fees). The upside is an unknown at this time. When the market traded up to the next master natural number of 12800, the trader could raise the sell stop to the next-lower natural number (12700, in this case). At this point, the risk on the trade was minimized to a small number, an approximate break-even, with the upside still open. When

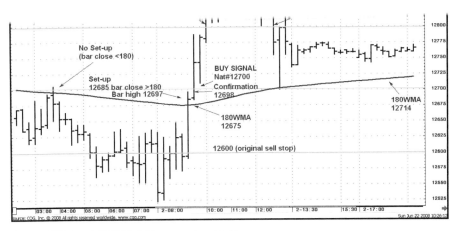

Chart 9.4 Buy signal example

The Sell Signal

The sell signal is the mirror image of the buy signal. First, the 180-period WMA line is calculated and drawn on a short-term chart.

Our program rules remain the same for a sell signal (mirror image):

N#M Rules: Sell Signal

Entering a new short requires three steps:

1. The setup
2. The confirmation
3. The sell signal

When the market trades below 12725 in this case, the oil market has now confirmed that the trend is down and is set up for a new sell signal at the next master natural number (in this case, 12700). Therefore, we would now place a sell stop to enter a new short position at 12700. If the market should again close above the moving average before the 12700 buy stop is hit, the setup for this sell signal is canceled and the process begins again. In this case, we wait for a new setup, confirmation, and sell (or buy) signal, with trade entry at the closest natural number. However, if the market trades down to 12700 in this example, we will automatically be stopped in a new short position. After being stopped in a new sell, the buy stop on this new short position will initially be placed at the closest higher natural number (in this case, 12800). After a new trade is executed, the stop will be trailed—for a sale, lowered one natural number every time a new lower natural number is exceeded below the market until the trend turns and the market takes us out. When we're out, we wait for the next setup, confirmation, and signal.

What Happens After a Trade Is Completed?

It's possible to generate a new signal in the same direction (what we call a *rebuy* or a *resell*), or a new reversal signal (opposite direction) can occur if the market reverses direction. It all depends on market action. If the previous trade was a buy signal and the market remains above the 180-period WMA, a new buy signal is generated at the next-higher natural number. In this case, no setup or confirmation is required—only a trade to the next-higher natural number. Or if the market continues lower and trades below the 180-period WMA, a new sell signal could potentially be generated (after a setup, confirmation, and trade to the next-lower natural number). After a trend is established via the setup-and-confirmation process, only trades in that direction can take place until a trend in the opposite direction is established via the setup-and-confirmation process. In this way, the natural number method takes advantage of a trend in an attempt to squeeze as much profit out of a long-lasting trend as possible. A trend remains

.... up to 11100, and subsequently raise it twice more on this chart. Looking at this chart, we do not know the ultimate outcome. The market might continue much higher before a 100-point break; however, we can see that the rebuy from 11300 is now sure to return at least an approximate 200-point profit (because the raised stop is now working at 11500). In conclusion, the first signal correctly identified the prevailing trend, but random market action stopped us at a loss. The rebuy bailed us out, and the two trades combined during this period resulted in a net profit.

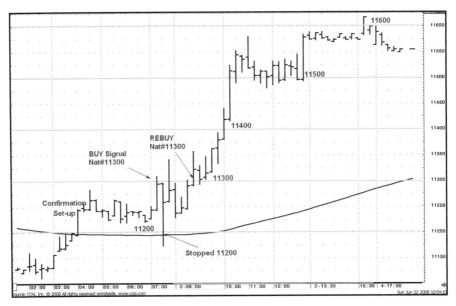

Chart 9.5   Rebuy example

are generally minor considerations). In a trending market, o.. upside per trade could be one, two, or three units, or many more. But the point is that the profit per trade is not capped at one unit—this could easily be multiple units. Bottom line: If we are always risking one unit but have the potential to realize multiple units on the profit side of the ledger, then even a 50/50 win-to-loss ratio will result in positive bottom-line profitability. And I've found that, in the long run, with the natural number trading system, a 50/50 or even greater win-to-loss ratio (the winning trades outperforming the losers) is the norm and not the exception.

In executing the program, remember that the moving average determines the trend. *When the market is trading above the average, only a new buy or a rebuy can be signaled. When the market is trading below the average, only a new sell or a resell can be signaled.* A short sale can never take place (regardless of market action) above the moving average line, and a buy cannot take place (regardless of market action) when the market is trading below the moving average line.

Now let's look at how the *natural number method* performs in a *real-time market situation.* One of the risk disclaimers is that past information is not a predictor of future market movements; however, with the N#M, we are using past market movements to determine the trend and then using current market data for entry signals.

What follows was not written in hindsight. It took place during the thick of the battle. We will follow the corn market beginning in March 2008 and ending in August 2008 with a blow-by-blow description of how to use the N#M during this period. I couldn't know beforehand how this market was going to perform. As I now know in writing this preview, the market action ended up taking place in different directions and didn't do what I—or anyone else, for that matter— could have expected during the period. Unlike many systems or methods you might see advertised, I didn't retrofit data to prove my theory. I had absolutely no idea how the bottom line would ultimately work out when we started on this journey in March. (I did it this way because it was an easier way for me to write

Why did I pick corn? I could have picked any volatile market. I picked corn only because it's a market I actively trade for clients and my own account. I have a commercial client who is a huge corn buyer, and I help with hedging strategies, but this has nothing to do with the N#M. The method is dynamic—you can easily apply it to any actively traded commodity. I knew 2008 had the potential for a major move in the corn market (due to lower planted acreage and new demand sources). As it turned out, other markets returned many more dollars per contract, and I could have shown you a more dramatic bottom line. However, corn worked out fine, with lower risk than other markets, and it was a good market to illustrate how the N#M works.

The Corn Campaign

Our journey begins in late-March 2008, a time when the USA corn crop, grown primarily in the Midwest, was in the early planting phase. How the market would perform this year would be based on myriad unknown factors at this time. How would the growing season unfold, both in the United States and internationally? What would the ultimate demand be for livestock feeding and industrial uses, such as ethanol and corn syrup?

Prices at this time were already trading at historic highs for any planting period, opening the way for a major bear move (if a large crop was ultimately realized) or a substantial bull move (should any weather problems develop).

Beginning our journey in mid-March, the corn market was in a bear trend, trading well under the 180-period weighted moving average (all charts are 30-minute bar charts). However, as shown in Chart 9.6, a 30-minute bar was able to close above the average on March 24, setting the market up for a buy signal at the next natural number (in this case, 540).

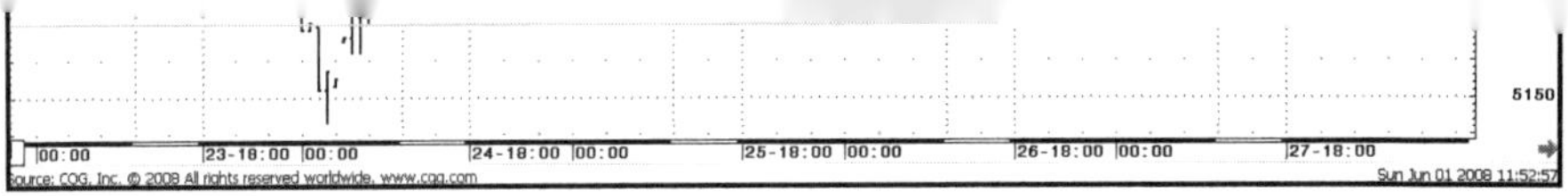

Chart 9.6   March 23–27 (corn 30-minute bar chart)

Let's look at this first buy signal, Trade 1, to illustrate how this all works.

Before the March 24 buy signal, the corn market was in a downtrend. How did we know this? Simple: The market was trading below the 180-period WMA, as shown in Chart 9.6. On the 12:30 PM Central Standard Time bar (this was 45 minutes before the closing bell), the market closed above the WMA at 539, setting up a potential buy signal (confirmed by trading above the high of the bar, or 539) at the next-higher natural number (in this case, 540). Our methodology involves placing our buy stop above the market (always place buy stops above the market and sell stops below) to enter a new long position at 540. If the market had faded into the close and again traded (and bar-closed) under the 180-period WMA, this setup would have been negated. However, in short order the market rallied up to 540, the buy stop was triggered, and a new long position was automatically entered. After the order was executed, our next order of business was to immediately place our protective sell stop to set our risk point on the trade. Our sell stop was placed good until canceled or replaced (GTC) at the next-lower natural number (in this case, 530, which is not shown in this zoomed-in chart). (See Chart 9.7.) At this time, our trade is placed in the hands of the "market gods"; we sit back, monitor the market, and see what unfolds.

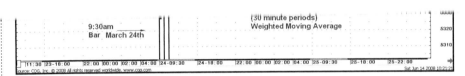

Source: CQG, Inc. © 2008 All rights reserved worldwide.

Chart 9.7　March 24 buy signal

This is what happened: The bull move continued, with the market rising to 560 on the 25th (when we moved our stop up one natural 10¢ unit, to 550) and again up to 570 on the 26th (when we again moved our stop up one unit to 560). The bull continued without a one-unit (10¢) retracement all the way up to 602 on the 31st. By this time, we had raised our stop to 590, and this was the stop point that was finally hit on the 31st during the 10:30 AM bar. On the recap spreadsheet at the end of this section, this is Trade 1.

Consider this summary of Trade 1, as shown in Chart 9.8: bought at 540 on March 24 and sold at 590 on March 31, with a resulting gain of 50 cents. Because one corn contract is sized at 5,000 bushels, every penny move in corn per contract represents a $50 profit or loss. In this case, we realized a $2,500 profit per contract on this trade. (The inevitable fees and any slippage are not included in our calculations—these generally amount to approximately 1¢ per contract or less.) Because we were risking one unit, which is 10¢, or $500 per contract, this represented a 5:1 profit-to-loss ratio on this first trade. Money management is automatic. Another way to look at this is that our next five signals in a row would all need to be losers to slip us into negative profitability. Although this is possible, the odds are against it. We are off to a good start.

Chart 9.8   March 27–April 1

Now we're out of the market. What next?

The first thing to note is that the market remains above the moving average, so at this point, we would take only a potential new buy signal (a rebuy). *Remember, when the market is trading above the average, only a new buy or a rebuy is able to be signaled.* The next natural number up is 600, so we would place a buy stop to reenter at 600.

However, the market doesn't move back up to 600. Instead, it continues to head south and trades under 580 (at which time we lower our reentry buy stop by one 10¢ unit to now enter at 590) and continues trading down as low as 570.5 (briefly trading under the average). At this point, if the market continued lower than 570 and the bar closed below the average (under 570), a potential new sell signal (most likely at 560) would have been set up. However, the market bounced off the average (a common occurrence in a trending market), with the bar closing at 581 near the closing bell on the 31st. This is what I call a *swing bar,* and I've identified it on Chart 9.9. This action set up a potential new buy signal (a rebuy) at the 590 level, which was hit the following trading session. This is Trade 2, a rebuy at 590. This trade was completed when the raised stop at 600 was hit on April 6 for a modest 10¢ profit.

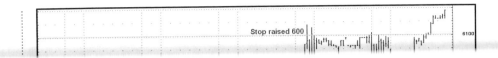

Chart 9.9 April 1–6

The majority of our trades, regardless of market, for the natural number method tend to result in a modest (one-unit) profit or loss, or a break-even. We know at the outset that our loss is essentially capped at one unit (or slightly above one unit, with slippage), but our upside per trade will be open. If the N#M has the capability to maintain our equity (our stake) during the quiet, sideways markets and enables us to capitalize on a few big winners during the trending periods (down or up), we'll prosper in the long run.

On April 7, the program signaled a new short sale at 600, with a reversal signal on the 9th at 610. The sell signal (Trade 3) resulted in a 10¢ loss (600 – 610 = –10). Subsequently, this turned into a reversal buy signal at 610 (Trade 4), with the raised stop hit overnight on the 10th at 610—the same price as entry for a break-even. See Chart 9.10 for a visual summary.

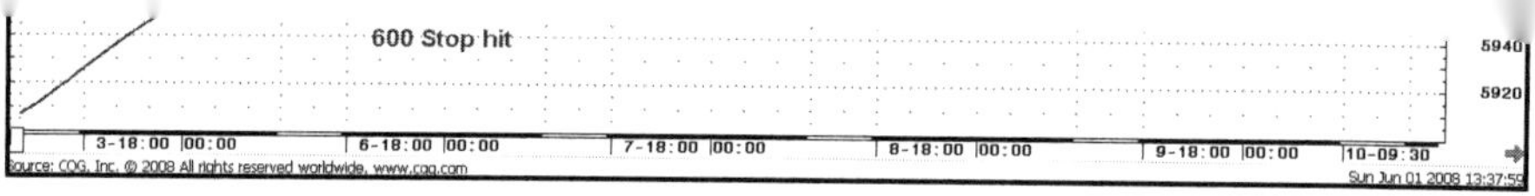
600 Stop hit
5940
5920
3-18:00 00:00
6-18:00 00:00
7-18:00 00:00
8-18:00 00:00
9-18:00 00:00
10-09:30
Source: CQG, Inc. © 2008 All rights reserved worldwide, www.cqg.com
Sun Jun 01 2008 13:37:59

Chart 9.10 April 3–10

The next trade (5) was a buy, signaled at 620 on the 14th. When the market crossed 630 on the 17th, we were able to raise our sell stop to 620. At this point, a break-even or small loss would be the worst result. Chart 9.11 shows the stop being hit on the 18th, with the market already set up for a reversal signal at 620.

Source: CQG, Inc. © 2008 All rights reserved worldwide.

Chart 9.11   April 14–21

On the 18th, Trade 6 was a new sell signal, at 620. The lowered stop at 610 hit overnight on the 21st for a 10¢ profit (short from 620, covered at 610 = +10).

Chart 9.12   April 21–27

The market continued to chop around. It set up at 618 but never reached the 620 natural buy signal point. Then it traded back below the moving average, set up for a sale at 605, but never reached the 600 natural sell signal point. On the

Chart 9.13   April 23–29

Chart 9.14 May 1–7

The March–May time period took place during planting. It was very wet in a large portion of the Midwest, and this slowed the planting progress. Farmers were having trouble getting their crops in the ground, particularly in the key growing states of Iowa, Minnesota, and Illinois. In late-April into May, they had approximately a two-week window to plant the corn. If the weather remained wet, a massive acreage shift to soybeans would occur. (Farmers can plant beans later in the season without appreciable yield loss.) The market chopped around, and in early May, certain analysts were calling for a move to 700 or higher.

However, the sun came out, the fields dried up, and the Midwestern farmers were able to get back in the fields and plant their corn crop. No follow-through for the bull market occurred during mid May—and Trade 11–12

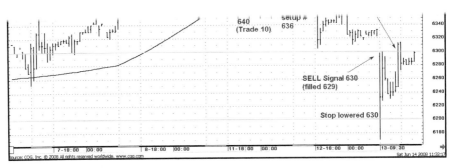

Chart 9.15   May 7–13

Trade 11 (on the left side of Chart 9.16) was a sell signal on the 13th and was stopped in short order for another break-even to small loss. (Due to slippage, the sell signal from 630 was actually filled at 629.) It was too bad this stop was hit (the market didn't go much higher that night) because the market then dropped another 20¢, resulting in a resell below the level where we were stopped. *Remember, when the market is trading below the average, only a new sell or a resell can be signaled.*

Chart 9.16   May 12–18

On the 21st, a new buy at 620 was stopped, and then the N#M reversed our direction at the same price on the 27th (see Chart 9.17). The market has been fairly tame for a few months now, and at this point, the book and the market are getting boring. I still believe corn will be a decent market to illustrate the N#M, but I am beginning to wonder if I shouldn't have picked a more dramatic market.

Source: CQG, Inc. © 2008 All rights reserved worldwide.

Chart 9.17   May 20–27

On May 30, the last trading day of the month, the market opened lower at 606 and began to rally (right side of Chart 9.18). Within minutes after the open, the lowered 610 stop was hit, for a 10¢ profit on the sell from the 27th (Trade 16). At 10:30 AM CST, the market set up at 610 and went to a new natural number buy at 620 by 12:30 PM. The market traded as high as 630 that Friday, closing at 626.5—up17¢ for the day. On June 2, the market traded above 640, enabling us to raise the stop to 630; however, this stop was hit on a correction to just below 630 on June 3.

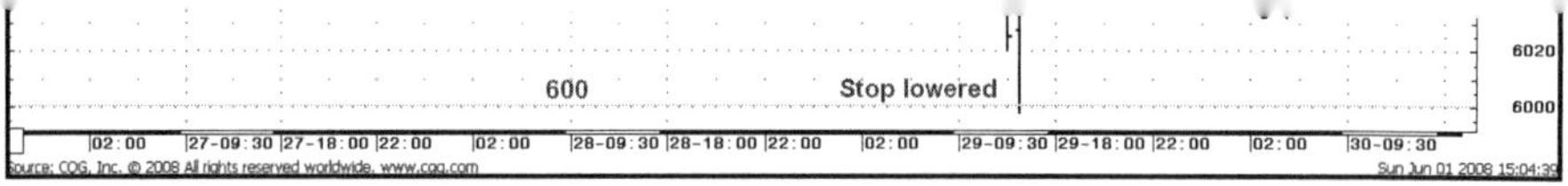

Chart 9.18   May 27–June 1

I hope you've been able to follow along to this point, although I realize this is becoming a bit tedious. But I thought it was important for you to see the ebb and flow of how signals are generated and acted upon. Now it will start to get more interesting.

At this point, in early June, we were out of the market waiting for the next signal. If the market had traded and closed under the moving average line, a new sell signal would have been generated at either 620 or 630 (depending on the placement of the 30-minute close in relation to the average line). However, the market remained above the moving average and instead traded back up to the natural number 640. Although the previous trade initially resulted in a 10¢ profit, it ultimately cost us 10¢. If the market had not traded down to 630 (actually to 629 1/2, a mere half-penny below), we would have still been in this trade instead of needing to buy back at 640.

A dramatic "weather rally" (the first of the season) ensued over the following weeks (see Chart 9.19). It continued to rain for a solid week, and 2 million to 3 million acres of corn remained unplanted. Many farmers were unable to move heavy equipment onto their saturated fields. Areas of Iowa experienced what were called the 200-year floods, and large portions of Indiana farmland were also drowned out. During the next week, corn continued to rally, hitting numerous new all-time highs and slicing through the natural numbers 670, 680, and 690. On June 6, the market experienced a 10¢ retracement. Our raised 680 ~~stop was offset with our previous 640 buy, resulting in a 40 point field and~~

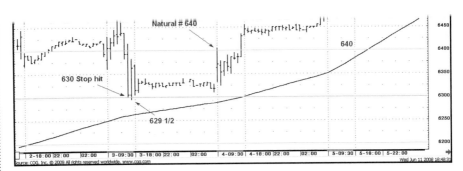

Chart 9.19   June 2–5

You can now begin to see how the natural number method is able to capture the bigger trending moves—those moves with the best profit potential. Remember that I didn't cherry-pick the corn market to show a good result for the book. I preselected corn to illustrate the trading method because I felt the market had the potential to make a move during the time I was writing this book, and it's a market that I trade actively anyway. I had no prior knowledge of how the market would trade before writing this chapter. As you will see, it all worked out nicely. But then again, after extensively testing and trading the method, I do have faith in it. It's dynamic, and it works over a wide variety of markets. Let me digress a bit at this point (we'll come back to the corn story) and show you the awesome potential the method has in the right situation. Certainly, this system has good and poor periods. It tends to work best in volatile or trending situations—where the big money is made. Sometimes it works spectacularly. If I cherry-picked an example to showcase the potential of

This was a period when oil, similar to corn, was registering all-time-high prices in a dramatic bull trend. The natural number method works exactly the same way for oil as it does for corn. The only difference is that we use a more sensitive 10-minute chart (for reasons that will be outlined later) versus the 30-minute chart we used for the corn market. The moving average is the same: 180-period weighted. The natural number for oil is the rounded dollar per barrel, 10000, or $100/barrel, 10100, or $101/barrel, 10200, or $102/barrel, and so forth. On June 5 oil crossed above the moving average line to generate a new buy signal at 12400, or $124 per barrel. A crude oil contact is for 1,000 barrels; therefore, every dollar move represents $1,000 profit or loss per contract traded. After the buy signal, the market ran up to 12700 in just a few hours. This amounted to an unrealized profit of $3,000 per contract traded—frankly, it would have been tempting to book the profit. However, the system had not backed us out, and, remember, the $3 move up enabled us to raise our stop to the next-lower natural number (in this case, 12600, or $126/barrel), thus ensuring an approximate $2,000 profit per contract traded. If we had accepted $3,000 profit per contract, however, we would have left something on the table.

Chart 9.20   June 5–6 oil

During the following 24 hours, this market ran another $6 before the first trailing stop was hit. Early the next morning, oil reached an unbelievable price (at that time) of $134 per barrel. At that point, our stop had been raised to $133, where it was hit for an incredible $9,000 profit on just one contract ($133 – $124 = 9 × $1,000). But wait—it was early on June 6 and if a trader had stuck to the program, he would have entered the rebuy at the 134 natural number and ridden this one up to 139. Then the trailing stop at 138 would have been hit for a second trade in two days, this one amounting to an additional $4,000 profit on each contract traded. Two signals in two days amounting to a gross profit of $13,000, or $130,000 for a 10-contract trader, $1.3 million for 100-contract trades, and so on. Certainly, this was a premier move, but trust me: Many more took place in oil and other markets this year, and plenty of others will occur in the future.

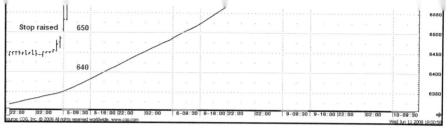

Chart 9.21   June 5–10

We are now out of the market, having accepted a 40¢ profit on Trade 18. At this point, we would reenter either on the short side after a new setup well below the market, or on a move back up to the next-higher natural number, 690. I suspected it would be a rebuy, and a new buy at 690 was triggered on Sunday evening (see Chart 9.22), June 8 (or at the open on Monday morning if the Sunday-evening market were not being monitored).

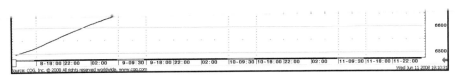

Source: CQG, Inc. © 2008 All rights reserved worldwide.

Chart 9.22   June 8–11

On Tuesday the 10th, corn futures traded above $7 per bushel (the 700 master natural number) for the first time in history. In classic Livermore fashion, December corn quickly ran up the 30¢ limit on June 11, enabling us to raise our stop three additional times and "locking in" an additional 30¢ profit during just that one trading session (Chart 9.23).

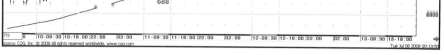

Chart 9.23   June 11–13

After the limit up move, the market was fairly wild. December corn traded up to a new all-time high above 750; then the market broke 20¢, stopping us out at 740. We received a fairly nice 50¢ gain, or $2,500 profit per contract.

Once again we could have gone either way, but it was a bull market. And after the move under 730, we again got stopped in on the long side at 740, raised the stop to 740 on the move to 750, and were stopped out at 740 (all in the same day). For those of you keeping score, we have just completed Trade 20. The sentiment was very bullish at this point in time, and nobody could have predicted what was to transpire in the coming few months.

Granted, Chart 9.23 has a lot going on, and if you're having trouble following it, perhaps now is a good time to review our rules. It's really quite systematic and fairly simple to execute the strategy when you understand the rules.

To review, after being sell-stopped out at 680 on June 6, the market rallied and we were buy-stopped into a new long position at the next-higher natural number (in this case, 690). From this buy point all the way up to 750, no 10¢ retracement occurred to stop us out of this long position. Every time the market rallied higher to reach a new higher natural number, we were able to raise our stop by 10¢. The first full 10¢ break came after the 750 natural number was reached, stopping us out at 740 and enabling us to accept a realized 50¢ profit on the 690 buy.

Now it's June 12 and we're flat (out of the market, with no position), waiting for the next signal. Once again, this turned out to be a buy at 740. The market then proceeded to rally and break back d——

19, the very day *Newsweek* ran a front-page cover photo of a flood victim up to his head in water. The market then proceeded to trade lower for the rest of that year. With all the bullish news, I wondered if the market was making a top or whether it could continue to surge higher yet.

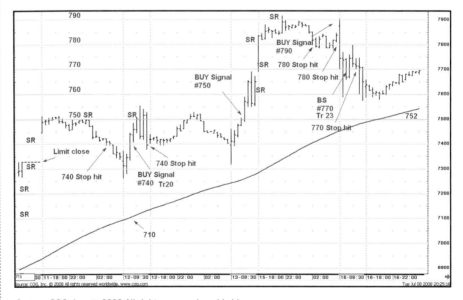

Chart 9.24   June 11–16

symptom of this phase. The beauty of NNM is its inherent a... ... .g.......

Even though we saw four times as many losses as profits during this two-week period, our drawdown was manageable. If you had consistently taken the signals in the previous few weeks, this drawdown came off profits.

This brings us to the question, "What is the recommended minimum account size to trade the natural number method?"

What if you had the unfortunate luck to start at the worst possible time (in this period that would have been Trade 22 on June 16)? Your drawdown would have been about $1,500 per contract traded (slightly higher if you add in fees and slippage). Even with a modest account, assuming you don't overtrade more contracts than the equity can handle during the down periods, a drawdown of this size is manageable. My recommendation is to trade one contract per signal for a market similar to corn (a risk of approximately $500 per contract per trade) for each $10,000 in equity. For markets in which the risk per trade is higher (risk per trade is discussed later in this chapter), I recommend a larger-sized account. For a market in which the projected risk per trade is $1,000 per contract, I recommend a $20,000 minimum account size. If your starting equity is $100,000, you then have the option to diversify, which I recommend. For example, trade five unrelated markets: three markets with a projected risk of $1,000 risk per contract per trade and two markets with a projected risk of $500 per contract per trade, with two contracts per trade.

Getting back to our corn campaign, we are now on a reversal buy (moved back from the short to the long side) for Trade 30, and although we didn't know it at the time the trade was entered, our drawdown period had ended. Since the campaign started about three months ago, this had been the worst cumulative drawdown period, still manageable for all but the very smallest of accounts.

Trade 30 resulted in a $1,000 profit but was literally inches away from generating a much larger profit. The market had an interim peak at the all-time high price of 799 1/4 that week, and if it had been just 75 higher, a 3/4 of

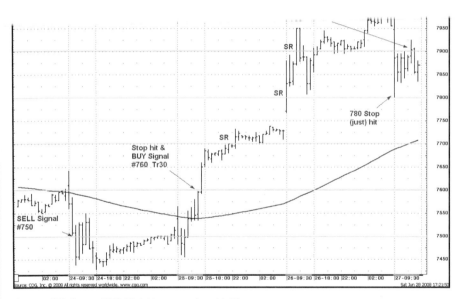

Chart 9.25   June 24–27

The Friday rebuy was unfortunate because it came before the crop report released on Monday, June 30. This report was released before the market opened and was a bearish shocker for corn. The government reported planted acreage at more than 87 million, which was above the March intentions number and a surprise to most traders (including me), who were looking for a big reduction in planted acres due to the flooding. The market gapped lower and our 780 stop was filled at 773 1/4, nearly 7¢ under the stop price. This is a good example of negative slippage, which occurs when a major surprise hits a market.

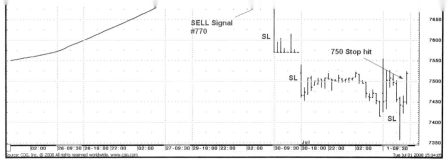

Source: CQG, Inc. © 2008 All rights reserved worldwide.

Chart 9.26   June 26–July 1

The market then moved higher, reversing to a new buy signal at 770 on July 2: Stop raised to 770, stop hit, rebuy at 780, and stop hit at 770 for a 10¢ loss in a volatile session. This was a classic test of the high that would ultimately fail with another rebuy and stop hit, for another 10¢ loss. This can be quite trying, particularly in a weather market scenario, and you need to be disciplined to stick with the program. Up to this point, the volatility had been remarkable considering the fact that weather markets generally don't even begin until after the July 4th holiday. After July 4 is often considered a pivot point for the corn market. This time period often points the way for the remainder of the summer. The trend this year had been up. Returning from the holiday, you would expect either a change in trend (if the market weakens from this area) or a continuation of the bull trend to new highs above $8 per bushel.

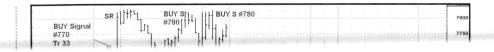

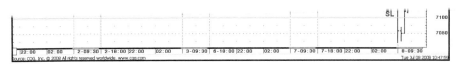

Source: CQG, Inc. © 2008 All rights reserved worldwide.

Chart 9.27   July 2–8

A change in trend is exactly what happened. On July 7 the first trading day after the July 4th holiday, the market opened sharply lower. Note how Trade 36 was triggered: The first setup was 749 1/2, under the 750 natural number, setting up a sell signal at the next-lower natural number of 740. However, the market proceeded to rally to 760; therefore, the next sell signal setup could actually be raised to 750 (the next lower natural number). If the market had traded above the 180-period WMA line, it could easily have set up for a new buy signal, most likely at 770. However, corn was heavy that day and sank back to 750 for a fresh sell signal. It closed that day at the 30¢ limit down level of 747. Apparently, the pivot was pointing south. The first 10¢ retracement from a natural number was on the 8th at 720, resulting in a 30¢ profit for that trade (see Chart 9.27).

Chart 9.28 July 9–11

What if a market gaps up or down above or below a natural number? If it has already set up, consider this your confirmation and take the trade at the market. Generally, a gap is caused by an unexpected event, such as a geopolitical event, a weather event, or an economic or crop report. For example, Trade 38 was triggered at the natural number 700 due to a gap open lower (caused by an inaccurate weather forecast—it was wet and cool, not hot and dry). This trade was filled at 696 and subsequently stopped at a small profit (after a sharp break that enabled the stop to be lowered to 690). In this case, the gap only led to a choppy trade that was stopped out for a small profit, followed by a resale for a loss and another resale at the same price for a 10¢ profit (see Chart 9.29).

However, pay attention to gap action because gaps sometimes signal the start of a major move.

Chart 9.29   July 11–16

Let me stress again that choppy periods will occur and will test your patience. You need to believe in the program and keep your faith to stick it out. This is where diversification can help; when one market is in a consolidation (sideways) pattern, another might be trending. As it turned out, during this period, when we were getting chopped up a bit in corn, other unrelated markets were trending nicely. For example, let's briefly digress again to the oil market. Remember that big bull move approximately a month earlier? On July 15, the oil market collapsed, and the program (we are using a 10-minute chart for oil) generated a sell signal that resulted in a $7,000 profit on just one contract *in less than one hour's trading* (with a maximum initial risk of $1,000). You now know how it works; Chart 9.30 shows what it looked like.

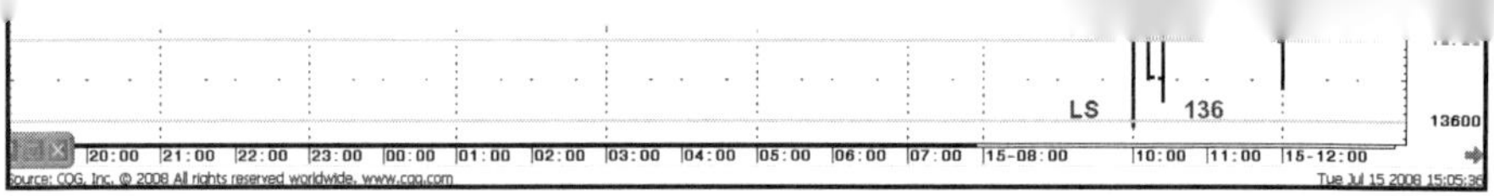

Chart 9.30   July 15 oil

Diversification

A few thoughts on diversification: When trading the natural number method, I recommend diversifying into a minimum of three unrelated markets. These markets should be broad and liquid, to allow for stop orders with minimal slippage. Although this rule is not written in stone and I believe that you can make money using this methodology trading just one or two markets, this generally takes longer and requires greater patience, particularly if you start at the wrong time. The premise is that the greater the diversification, the greater the chance of catching a major move *somewhere*. At any point in time, one market might be in a major uptrend and one might be in a major downtrend, with a third trendless. N#M works because the major moves will be profitable enough to offset the inevitable smaller losses inherent in those choppy market situations. The odds of catching major moves increase with the number of markets traded. One caveat: *They should be unrelated markets.* Although the Swiss franc and the euro can move in opposite directions sometimes, they generally move in the same direction (albeit at different speeds) in relation to the dollar. Soybeans and soybean oil can move in opposite directions (and they sometimes have, in the short run), but because they are directly related products,

the Japanese yen) work well. I also prefer to trade a grain, and I personally prefer soybeans (technically not a grain, but an oilseed) or corn because they both can trend nicely and possess sufficient volatility. Finally, I recommend that you consider rounding off your portfolio with a metal (my personal preference is gold) and a financial, such as a stock index or interest-rate product.

The natural number method is dynamic—theoretically, it works over time if used systematically on a variety of unrelated markets or any single market. However, my experience has been that thin markets, such as lumber and platinum, place the odds against us at the start because the fills will often be disappointing.

Sometimes our stops will *just* be hit and sometimes they will *just* be missed. As examples, Trade 41 (a resell from 670; see Chart 9.31) appeared to be one of those trades doomed from the start because the market immediately went the wrong way, trading as high as 679 1/2. Just as it appeared we would be stopped on this trade at a loss, the market headed south again, and the trade resulted in a 10¢ profit. It didn't go much above the 660 (lowered) stop before crashing another 90¢, with the next new short sale signaled at 650 (see Chart 9.31). Bottom line: These "justs" (just getting stopped, just missing a profit) appear to even out over time. It's a function of the "market gods" and is not within our control.

Chart 9.31   July 16–22

Trade 42 turned out to be our best trade of the campaign. We were able to lower the stop eight times before finally being stopped out on the 23rd at 580 (see Charts 9.31 & 9.32). The result was $3,500 profit per contract taking place in only five trading days. With the floods in the news a few weeks ago, who would have thought our best trade to date would be from the short side? The news this time was "perfect weather," with (this coming almost out of thin air) a bountiful corn crop in development, the flood-ravaged crop of the previous month seemingly forgotten. The truth is, the majority of analysts we followed did not see this route coming. This big bear move was partially in sympathy, with a broadly based commodity sell-down (lead by weak oil during this period), and also largely created by margin-call selling. Once again, as Soros has taught us, money became the most important fundamental. The natural number method is not concerned with fundamentals—only market action; the market action led us by using N#M to sell when scores of others were buying—and it worked.

Chart 9.32   July 21–25

After a major move, the market will often consolidate. The market did become choppy again, resulting in the inevitable whipsaw with two 10¢ losing trades in quick succession. On July 25, the program generated its first new buy signal since July 3. At this point, we have no way of knowing whether this will be the start of a new bull trend or whether the consolidation will continue. We see indications that the bear move might have run its course. However, after the July 25 signal, the weather forecast was constantly changing from perfect to hot, but plenty of rain mitigated the heat, and the conditions remained good. The market chopped back and forth with the changing weather forecasts. Trades 44–48 (not pictured) did not help us with three losses, one break-even, and one profit during this choppy period.

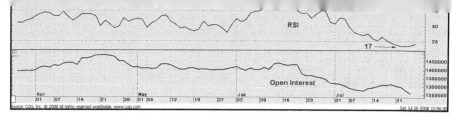

Chart 9.33   Daily corn (late-March–late-July)

Looking at the daily chart for the period during this corn campaign, we can now see that this crop year exhibited all three possible trend scenarios. The April–May period was a sideways trend, June exhibited a classic uptrend, and July was a classic downtrend. This is all easy to see in hindsight. As the saying goes, "Hindsight is always 20/20"—however, in the thick of the battle, it's not always easy to determine the major trend. The overall profitability that has been demonstrated throughout all three scenarios is a testament to the power of the N#M.

As we apply it, the N#M works on a shorter-term time frame. Because of the volatility that results from electronic trading, I advocate using a shorter-term time frame for trading. However, I am not suggesting that you rely on just a single indicator. Analyzing the market in the context of longer-term time frames and alternative technical indicators will assist our trading and enhance profitability.

Let's now briefly discuss using the 50-day EMA, the RSI, and Open Interest to improve your analysis and supplement the N#M. But first let me draw your attention to the master natural numbers 600 and 700.

discuss 600 first. On April 2, 2008, the actively traded December corn contract broke above 600 and closed at 603—the first close above 600 in the history of corn futures trading. Take a look at how 600 then acted as major support. For the following two months, although the market essentially moved sideways, this number acted as a major support, with the market continually bouncing off this master number. Until the market embarked on the next major leg higher in June, it was never again able to close under 600. Then on June 10, for the first time in the history of corn futures trading, the market broke above 700, closing at 702 3/4. This was a classic Livermore-type signal. If he were alive and trading, Livermore would have no doubt been a buyer on that first close above this master natural number. During the next trading session, the market gapped sharply higher (it opened at 715) and never looked back. The next-higher master natural number was 800. I have no doubt that this number will be breached at some point in the future; however, at the date of this writing, 800 ($8 per bushel) has not been traded on the U.S. corn futures market. The all-time high price remains 799 1/4 (traded on the electronic market). So if you buy our theory, waiting for a breach of 800 to buy at that level saved us from buying at a high. When 700 was exceeded, the old rule that former resistance should act as support came into play. Therefore, you would expect 700 to hold on the correction. However, on July 14, the pit-traded corn *gapped below* 700 to open at 684. If you were trading the electronic market that evening, you would have been a step up on this new short sale (or liquidating a stale long position) on an exit (long) or entry (short) on the break below 700. However, even if you had waited for the pit market to confirm weakness, selling on this open (the sharp gap below 700) proved to be the right move. During the next seven trading sessions, the market traded sharply lower, almost in a straight line, ending below the Appendix, "A Moving Average Primer, an Open Interest Primer, and the Advanced Open Interest Course.") In Chart 9.33, the market remained above the 50-day EMA on a closing basis during the first 13 weeks of this chart. May 29 was the only day during this period when it traded below, but it was able to close "above the line" on that day. It is no coincidence that the market was primarily in an uptrend during this period. After the market closed below the 50-day EMA, the market continued lower in almost a straight line. This is a lagging indicator, and we can see in hindsight that the market had peaked June 27 at just below $8. It didn't close below the 50-day EMA until July 14 at below $7. Our N#M is much more sensitive. (It moved into sell mode on July 7 at $7.50.) Still, the 50-day EMA (as well as other longer-term averages) is worth charting on a daily basis to provide additional evidence of the major trend and help place us on the right side of the market.

The RSI

The RSI is a useful tool that is popular with traders as an *overbought* or *oversold* indicator. Welles Wilder developed the RSI in the late-1970s. You'll hear brokers, advisory firms, newsletters, and others touting the words *oversold* and *overbought*. This is what they're talking about: Markets don't go straight up or straight down forever without corrective moves. A point comes when the market is ready to turn and change trend (or correct if still within a major trend) because the buying or selling has been temporarily satiated. *Overbought* basically means the market is too high and is running out of buyers for the move—ready to fall from its own weight. *Oversold* is the reverse: The market is too low for the move, running out of sellers (at least, for the current time period) and ready for a bounce. These are not very scientific terms and are used arbitrarily. The RSI attempts to statistically quantify the degree to which a market is overbought or oversold.

than 75. How do you use the RSI? When this number gets too small or too big, it is theoretically time to put up your antenna. The market is getting close to a reversal point. Some traders attempt to buy when the RSI wanders into the oversold range and sell in the overbought range. My opinion is that if you attempt to do this, you'd better have deep pockets. Sometimes (for example, in trading-range type markets) this *can* be an excellent way to pick tops and bottoms. However, in the major moves and at extremes (the most profitable time for the trend follower), the RSI can remain in the extreme ranges for long periods of time and for potentially large moves. This is the major drawback of the RSI. It works in normal markets, but when the market is in the blow-off or panic stage, it can remain in overbought or oversold territory for an extended period and can become quite costly.

Still, I think the RSI can be a useful tool, particularly when used in conjunction with other indicators and the N#M. You need to know what type of market you are in (trading-range or trending, young or mature). If you can determine this, the RSI can help you identify what point in the life cycle of the market you're at. RSIs tend to get high in the mature stages of a bull market and low in the mature stages of a bear market, but no magic number signals the bottom. In fact, I've found it is better practice to watch for the RSI to turn up *after* it falls under 25 to signal a bottom, and vice versa for the bull. Yet even this tactic tends to lead to numerous false and money-losing signals because the RSI is a *coincident* indicator: It moves with price. A minor upswing has to turn the RSI up.

As I suggested in my previous books, the best way to use RSI is to look for *divergences*. These occur when the RSI doesn't make a new low or a new high coincidentally with the market. For example, let's suppose coffee rallies from 128 to 158; the RSI registers a high for the move of 83 at 158 (so it is in moved into overbought territory (above 75) on June 9 at 685. We can put up our antenna, but the trend remained strongly up, and the RSI continued to move higher with the market. The RSI peaked at an extremely high overbought reading of 90 on June 18 at a closing price of 780, and the market made a higher high on June 26–27, with the RSI showing divergence (lower reading of 75). The RSI worked beautifully in this case, signaling the top well before other indicators. The market and the RSI then both proceeded to move lower, with the RSI first reaching oversold territory below 25 on July 18 (close of 628 1/2). The RSI reached a low of 17 on July 22 at 592. At this point in time, we have no way of knowing whether the low for the move has been registered; however, the oversold reading has our antenna up looking for other indicators to confirm that the low is, in fact, in. Our first new buy for the N#M in 22 days came on July 25 at major number 600, and we can see other clues that a new bull trend might potentially be in its infancy. Bottom line: I have found the RSI to be an extremely useful tool and recommend that you add it to your technical toolbox, particularly because it provides information the lagging indicators can't.

Open Interest (OI)

This is a powerful technical forecasting tool available only to futures trades. For a full discussion of what open interest is and how it works (including my six profit rules for analyzing open interest), see the appendix.

In Chart 9.34, open interest did provide valuable forecasting information. It peaked on June 13 at 1,433,923 contracts (labeled as the OI peak). The close on that date was 765. The market continued to rally until June 27 (as high as 799 1/2 in the electronic market and 796 in the pit market); however, during this last surge to new highs, OI was falling (down almost 100,000 contracts to 1,343,348 on that date). This is my Rule 3: *If prices are in an uptrend and open interest is falling, this is a bearish sign.* OI analysis gave us an excellent warning

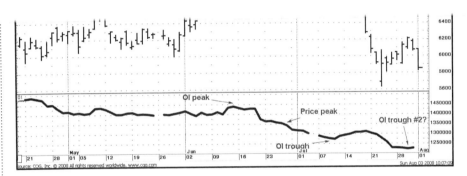

Chart 9.34   Daily corn (May–July) with OI

OI then continued to fall, bottoming on June 10 at 1,273,928. (This is labeled the OI trough.) On this date, the market had fallen about a dollar from the top, with about 160,000 contracts liquidated out, but then OI once again began to rise. If the market had turned back up, this would have been a bullish sign; *however, it continued lower while OI rose.* This was an excellent bearish indication, as outlined in my Rule 2: *If prices are in a downtrend and open interest is rising, this is a bearish sign.*

This rise in OI peaked on July 18 at 1,313,707 and then declined to new lows by the end of the chart (the end of July). According to Rule 4, this is a bullish leading indicator: *If prices are in a downtrend and open interest is falling, this is a bullish leading indicator.* However, this is just a leading indicator and can be off by weeks. (Rule 4 was a great leading indictor of the top, but it took two weeks of declining OI before the top was made.) We would like to see evidence of Rule 1 to indicate that the bottom is, in fact, in place. However, mentals are logical—but the market is always right.

This is what actually happened (as shown in Chart 9.35): Trade 48 was a sell signal at the master natural number 600. It lasted for a mere three trading days, but it was good for a 50¢ profit from the short side during that time—another 50¢ taken out of the short side from a market that had already dropped 200¢, proving once again that the method was smarter than I was.

Chart 9.35   August 1–7

The market turned choppy during the following week, with four resells—two for 10¢ profits and two for 10¢ losses.

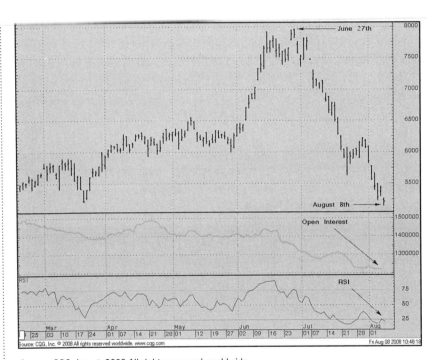

Figure 9.36 Daily corn chart ending August 8

The RSI remained oversold and was showing some evidence of divergence (seen at the bottoms), but the N#M remained in a sell mode. (The next setup at this time was above the market, at 540.) OI Rule 4 still told us to be alert for a bottom at any time, plus a major crop report was due out on August 12. Before the crop report, N#M has us flat, out of the market.

Chart 9.37   August 11–14

Remember the August 11, 1995, bearish crop report that led me to construct my significant news indicator? This is the same August report, 13 years later. The close on the day before this crop report was 517; therefore, this number became our SNI (see Chart 9.38).

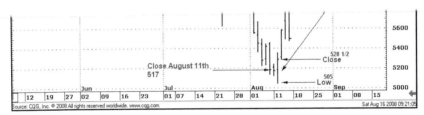

Source: CQG, Inc. © 2008 All rights reserved worldwide.

Chart 9.38   December 2008 corn (daily through August 14)

After the release of this very bearish report, the market traded to new lows for the campaign early in the session, down to 505. However, as soon as the market crossed above 517 (our SNI), this was a bullish signal. Our stop had already been hit on Trade 54 (the short from 510), and that day the market closed at 528 1/2. N#M signaled a new buy the next day at 540, with the market subsequently closing up the 30¢ limit that day and adding another 19¢ the following day. Bottom line: The SNI, with virtually zero risk, offered the potential for more than 60¢ ($3,000 per contract] profit in just a few days.

Summary

The corn campaign began in late March when I began to write this chapter. It's now mid-August and near my editor's deadline, so it's a good time to recap where we've been and how the N#M performed overall. It actually performed splendidly (we'll get to the actual numbers shortly), but first a review.

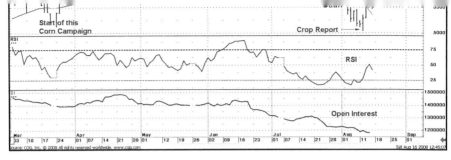

Chart 9.39   Corn campaign (daily summary)

At the time this is being written, about three months remain to trade this particular contract. However, it's deadline time for my publisher and, therefore, time to conclude our commentary for the corn campaign to date. Table 9.1 shows the results, summarized on a trade-by-trade basis.

Table 9.1 Corn Campaign Track Record

Trade#	Entry Date	Signal	Price	Exit Date	Price	P&L¢
1	24 Mar	BUY	540	31 Mar	590	50
2	1 Apr	REBUY	590	6 Apr	600	10
3	7 Apr	SELL	600	9 Apr	610	−10
4	9 Apr	BUY	610	10 Apr	610	0
5	14 Apr	REBUY	620	18 Apr	620	0
6	18 Apr	SELL	620	21 Apr	610	10
7	23 Apr	RESELL	610	24 Apr	610	0
8	27 Apr	BUY	620	29 Apr	630	10
9	5 May	SELL	620	6 May	620	0
10	7 May	BUY	630	12 May	640	10
11	13 May	SELL	629	14 May	630	−1
12	14 May	RESELL	620	15 May	620	0
13	16 May	BUY	630	16 May	620	−10
14	16 May	SELL	620	20 May	620	0
15	21 May	BUY	620	27 May	620	0
16	27 May	SELL	620	30 May	610	10
17	30 May	BUY	620	3 Jun	630	10
18	4 Jun	REBUY	640	6 Jun	680	40

Table 9.1 Continued

Trade#	Entry Date	Signal	Price	Exit Date	Price	P&L¢
19	9 Jun	REBUY	690	12 Jun	740	50
20	12 Jun	REBUY	740	12 Jun	740	0
21	13 Jun	REBUY	750	16 Jun	780	40
22	16 Jun	REBUY	790	16 Jun	780	−10
23	16 Jun	REBUY	770	16 Jun	770	0
24	17 Jun	REBUY	770	17 Jun	760	−10
25	17 Jun	REBUY	770	8 Jul	770	0
26	18 Jul	REBUY	780	19 Jun	770	−10
27	19 Jun	SELL	770	20 Jul	770	0
28	20 Jun	RESELL	760	23 Jun	750	10
29	24 Jun	RESELL	750	25 Jun	760	−10
30	25 Jun	BUY	760	27 Jun	780	20
31	27 Jun	REBUY	790	30 Jun	773	−17
32	30 Jun	SELL	770	1 Jul	750	20
33	2 Jul	BUY	770	2 Jul	770	0
34	3 Jul	REBUY	780	3 Jul	770	−10
35	3 Jul	REBUY	780	3 Jul	770	−10
36	7 Jul	SELL	750	8 Jul	720	30
37	9 Jul	RESELL	710	11 Jul	710	0

Trade#	Entry Date	Signal	Price	Exit Date	Price	P&L¢
38	13 Jul	RESELL	696	14 Jul	690	6
39	14 Jul	RESELL	680	15 Jul	690	–10
40	15 Jul	RESELL	680	16 Jul	670	10
41	17 Jul	RESELL	670	17 Jul	660	10
42	17 Jul	RESELL	650	23 Jul	580	70
43	23 Jul	RESELL	590	23 Jul	600	–10
44	24 Jul	RESELL	590	25 Jul	600	–10
45	25 Jul	BUY	600	28 Jul	600	0
46	29 Jul	SELL	590	29 Jul	600	–10
47	29 Jul	BUY	600	30 Jul	610	10
48	30 Jul	REBUY	620	31 Jul	610	–10
49	1 Aug	SELL	600	5 Aug	550	50
50	5 Aug	RESELL	540	5 Aug	550	–10
51	5 Aug	RESELL	550	7 Aug	540	10
52	8 Aug	RESELL	530	11 Aug	520	10
53	12 Aug	RESELL	510	12 Aug	520	–10
54	13 Aug	BUY	540	14 Aug	560	20
55	14 Aug	REBUY	560	15 Aug	560	0

sharp differences frequently arise between hypothetical performance results and the actual results subsequently achieved by any particular trading program. One of the limitations of hypothetical performance results is that they are generally prepared with the benefit of hindsight. In addition, hypothetical trading does not involve financial risk, and no hypothetical trading record can completely account for the impact of financial risk in actual trading. For example, the ability to withstand losses or to adhere to a particular trading program in spite of trading losses is a material point that can also adversely affect actual trading results. Numerous other factors related to the markets in general or to the implementation of any specific trading program cannot be fully accounted for in the preparation of hypothetical performance results, but they can adversely affect actual trading results.

The return-per-contract dollar figure on closed trades is based on one contract only. If you trade multiple contracts, multiply this number accordingly. The dollar figure is a gross profit or loss per single contract. (Commissions and any other fees are not subtracted because they would vary by trader.) Bottom line: I think I have fairly presented the gross returns (sans fees) that could actually be obtained; however, results could vary. Remember that it is impossible for me or anyone to guarantee the future because we are largely dealing with the unknown. Read the earlier risk disclaimer again; if you are uncomfortable with the risks involved here, you should not be doing this.

As of the end of the campaign, the margin required to trade one corn contract was $2,025. Therefore, based on margin, or even an account of nominal size, you might agree that $17,400 gross profit (minus commissions and fees) is an excellent return for a single contract traded over a period of less than half a year.

Additional Trading Points for N#M

volatile than sugar. This is partly a function of price, but also a function of each market's players. The more speculative the market, the more attractive it becomes to higher-risk speculators. Additionally, volatility can increase or decrease for the same market at different times, depending on conditions. Bottom line: Volatility changes and the more volatile markets today could fall out of speculative favor tomorrow. For these reasons, our time bar for the short-term chart is variable, and we constantly need to monitor the markets we trade for indications of volatility changes.

I've developed a general guide to help you determine the correct time interval to use for the N#M. This guide is based on the dollar value of the daily price range—a direct measure of volatility.

Time Interval Guide

If the dollar value of the daily price range per contract is

- $500–$749—Use a 45-minute chart.
- $750–$999—Use a 30-minute chart.
- $1,000–$1,499—Use a 25-minute chart.
- $1,500–$1,999—Use a 20-minute chart.
- $2,000–$2,999—Use a 15-minute chart.
- $3,000–$3,999—Use a 12-minute chart.
- **More than $4,000**—Use a 10-minute chart.

Determining the proper time interval requires approximately one month's (20–21 trading sessions) price data.

4 Mar	580	556.25	23.75
5 Mar	584	569.5	14.5
6 Mar	581.25	570.25	11
7 Mar	568.5	559.25	9.25
10 Mar	579.25	541	38.25
11 Mar	590	573.5	16.5
12 Mar	585	572.5	12.5
13 Mar	590	573.75	16.25
14 Mar	588.25	564	24.25
17 Mar	583.25	555	28.25
18 Mar	563.75	541.5	22.25
19 Mar	562.25	541.25	21
20 Mar	539.5	521.25	18.25
24 Mar	540.5	525.5	15
25 Mar	559.75	540	19.75
26 Mar	575	561	14
27 Mar	571.5	562.5	9
28 Mar	578	562.5	15.5
31 Mar	601	570	31
Average			18.63

One corn contract is sized at 5,000 bushels. Therefore, every penny-per-bushel move has a dollar value of $50 per contract. The average range during this period

20 May	13345	13224	121
27 May	13360	12828	532
28 May	13146	12612	534
29 May	13314	12630	684
30 May	12844	12487	357
2 Jun	12953	12542	411
3 Jun	12824	12425	399
4 Jun	12536	12216	320
5 Jun	12870	12205	665
6 Jun	13922	12814	1108
9 Jun	13869	13336	533
10 Jun	13838	13133	705
11 Jun	13885	13191	694
12 Jun	13809	13225	584
13 Jun	13762	13412	350
16 Jun	14042	13357	685
17 Jun	13591	13267	324
18 Jun	13734	13241	493
19 Jun	13836	13209	627
20 Jun	13750	13175	575
23 Jun	13814	13405	409
Average			545

Some common sense is required here. It would be unworkable if we used every subsequent natural number for a market with a large daily range because it would generate too many signals. In the oil market, natural numbers occur at every 10¢ per barrel level—for example 11800, 11810, and 11820. Ten cents is the equivalent of a $100-per-contract move for oil, but 10¢ for corn is the equivalent of a $500-per-contract move.

The general rule of thumb is that the break point should be no less than $500 per contract and no greater than $1,000 per contract. For shorter-term intervals (the more volatile markets), we generally would use the $1,000 break points. You certainly can modify these risk parameters, but, personally, I don't want to risk more than $1,000 (plus fees and slippage) per contract per trade. Therefore, I suggest that you use a maximum $1,000 break point for the most volatile markets (shorter time intervals). In the case of oil, this works out to be the master natural numbers—those that end in two zeros. Gold, as another example at the time of this writing, would use the $1,000 break point (930, 920, 910, and so on) and a 15-minute chart (see Charts 9.40 and 9.41).

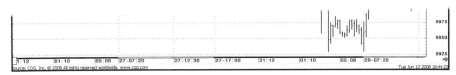

Chart 9.40   May 27–28 (August gold 15-minute chart)

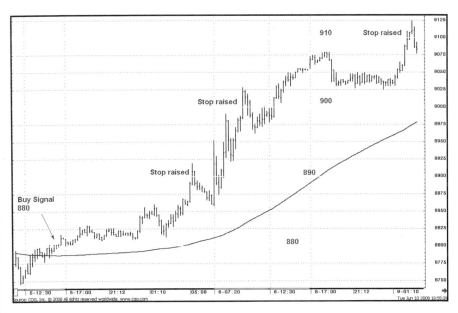

Chart 9.41   June 5–9 (August gold 15-minute chart)

you would place your sell stop at the next-lower master natural number (in this case, 11500). If filled, the initial buy stop is placed at 11600 and lowered to 11500 on a move down to 11400. This formula works for most markets because most futures markets are based on tens. However, what about a market such as copper, where one point equals $2.50? For copper, the most recent 30-day data at this writing indicates a daily range of just below 1,000 points. Because one point in copper equals $2.50, this is a $2,500 average range. Half of $2,500 is $1,250, and because this is above $1,000, we would use the $1,000 break point. For copper, this is 400 points (32500, 32900, and 33300). Therefore, we would use the next-closest natural number after the setup and confirmation with 400-point breaks. For example, if copper confirmed a buy signal at 34320, entry would be on a move up to the next-higher master natural number, or 34400. After entry, the initial stop would be 34000, with the first stop raise (to 34400) taking place if the market traded up to 34800, then the next stop raise at 35200, and so forth.

I have found this guide to be useful in my own trading; however, feel free to vary the intervals to suit your own style of trading. The important point to remember is that as volatility speeds up, your time interval shortens.

Improvements—Should Judgment Ever Be Used?

To accurately evaluate the methodology statistically, it was necessary to adhere to rigid rules. However, with some common sense and good judgment, it's certainly possible to improve our results. Consider these two possible situations in which you might have opted to use judgment to either lessen the risk or enhance the profit potential on a particular trade.

Entering or Exiting Early When Close to the Natural Number

It's generally not a good procedure to change the rules in the middle of a ...

... tip ... ... the key reversal higher, the bullish RSI readings, and our SNI flashing a buy signal), it made sense to enter immediately on the setup and not wait for the confirmation and buy signal. This action would have resulted in nearly a $1,500-per-contract profit versus $1,000.

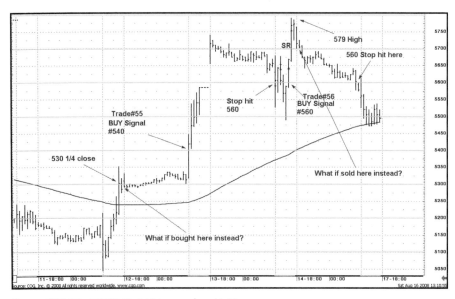

Source: CQG, Inc. © 2008 All rights reserved worldwide.

Chart 9.42   Improvements—Trades 55 and 56

As my deadline time approaches, the December contract still has more than three months to run, but another three months of blow-by-blow really isn't necessary; I think you got the idea here. Certainly, I'll continue to trade corn during this period, and my plan is to maintain the profit-and-loss data for the entire corn campaign (up until the delivery period at the end of November). If you're interested in learning how the corn campaign performed into the final months, I invite you to e-mail me at gkleinman1@mac.com. Additionally, I'm interested in hearing about your experiences with N#M and whether you've modified what I've presented in *The New Commodity Trading Guide*.

I sincerely hope you'll be able to use N#M to your benefit, and I wish you a very successful trading experience.

chapter 10

"It's a dog-eat-dog world, and I'm wearing Milk-Bone underwear."
—Norm (from *Cheers*)

"Chaos is a friend of mine."
—Bob Dylan

More than five decades ago, the legendary trader W. D. Gann described a market top:

> [Market tops are chaotic] with wild fluctuations, high volume and great activity; a feverish public buys madly; people wait for reactions, get discouraged, and buy at the market; fortunes are made in paper profits, yet less than 10% will ever cash in. The first sign of the end comes with a sharp break on no news (possibly at the open). This is the warning. Then a second rally may come to approximately the high point and could hold for awhile but THE SATURATION POINT IS REACHED; THE END IS NEAR; EVERYONE IS LOADED AND WILL BE LOOKING FOR A BUYER WHO IS NOWHERE TO BE FOUND. Then comes the deluge! At tops, HOPE & FEAR INCREASE TO THEIR HIGHEST LEVEL (and most people trade on hope & fear and not sound judgment). DO NOT WAIT UNTIL EVERYONE ELSE IS SELLING; GET OUT ON THE FIRST DANGER SIGNAL. When everyone wants to sell, profits run into losses fast. Profits from a whole year can be lost in days! WILD ACTIVE MARKETS ARE BROUGHT

other bastard die for his.

Today's electronic marketplace has a big problem. (Or is it an opportunity?) Critics say that the olden days of the pits added order to the markets. The professional market maker standing in the pit would observe the order flow in terms of the news, and he or she often took the other side of excessive speculative order flow. This made for a more orderly market environment. Many computer traders don't look at the news—they're looking at the trend of the market and hop on for the ride. Liquidation works the same way in reverse as they scramble out. Stops are hit, generating margin calls and causing more liquidation as it all feeds on itself. Without the professional market maker, this leads to vacuums and overextended moves because fewer players exist to take the other side of momentum. When the vacuum is finally filled, the move in the opposite direction is just as frenzied. Screen trading moves markets faster and takes them farther than the olden days, when the seasoned pit traders would step in front of the train.

Today's electronic markets are akin to a battlefield. Therefore, heed the words of Napoleon Bonaparte: "The battlefield is a scene of constant chaos. The winner will be the one who controls that chaos, both his own and the enemy's."

Today volatility is huge. Previously, "news days" were often volatile, but now we see volatility almost every day. We get instant fills now—a good thing—but in the process, the Internet has created a dog-eat-dog trading world. Get used to this because it's not going away. The good news is that the more extreme the moves, the better it is for our trend-following ways. And similar to the days of the pits, screen markets are also made by humans, and humans continue to respond to the same stimuli (natural numbers being one of them).

I've tried to provide you with some ideas and strategies to help you capture your fair share of the profit pool. As an old-time trader once told me, the key to success in trading is "Slow and steady wins the race." This requires calmness at all times, which is not always easy to obtain, but a systematic approach will help

the patience to hold tight.

It's equally important that you develop Gann's second essential quality of discipline: the discipline to take all the signals, including those that at first blush appear to be dead wrong. You need discipline and patience to stay with the winning trades until you have a definitive signal to exit. It's fun to take a profit, but taking premature profits will lead to ultimate failure. The impulse to take profits and try to reposition better will often be quite strong. You will see numerous times when a market is overdone, and you know you can reenter better if you cash in now. When this impulse hits you and you don't go with it, you'll often regret it. If you stick with your methodology and don't liquidate, you'll become frustrated if the market did what your gut said it would. Then the temptation becomes even greater to gut-trade the system next time. However, trust me: This is no recipe for success over the long run. The reason has to do with the nature of the big moves. When using a trend-following program, the best trades will be those you'll have the good fortune to be on for the longest periods of time. I'd consider our N#M corn campaign a success, but consider this: From more than 50 trades, just 6 of these generated more than 80% of the profits. Only about 10% of the trades generated 80% of the profits, and if you missed just one of these trades, you greatly impacted the bottom line. Before taking each signal, it was virtually impossible to know which of the trades would be the big money makers. If we could know, we'd make only those trades. But we're often dealing with the unknown. Also remember that, in an accelerating market, the most dramatic portion of the move generally takes place at the end. This is when your greatest profits accumulate and the temptation grows to book them prematurely. But you already know it's my contention that nobody alive is able to consistently pick the actual top or bottom. Discipline and patience, not brains or logic, will get you paid.

Finally, I would be pleased to hear from you. If you would like to share your experiences with N#M, or any interesting trading experience, for that matter, I'm all ears. If you believe you've developed an improvement for N#M or you would like to run your own program by me, I would like to hear about this as well. And if you have an interest in having me manage a trading account on your behalf, or if you have other market-related questions, shoot me an e-mail at geo@commodity.com, and I will do my best to respond in a timely manner.

It's easier paddling downstream than up, it takes less effort walking with the wind than into it, and it's our belief that it's more profitable trading with the trend than against it. It's difficult to be on the wrong side of a major move when you're on the right side of the trend.

Interest Course

"The market can remain irrational longer than you can remain solvent."
—Lord Keynes

Much of the appendix content was reproduced from my previous book, *Trading Commodities and Financial Futures: A Step-by-Step Guide to Mastering the Markets* (Upper Saddle River, NJ: Financial Times, 2004).

Section 1: A Moving Average Primer

If a Holy Trading Grail exists, I have not found it—and why would "they" (whoever "they" are) share it with you anyway? One of the most important lessons I can teach you is this: No single pattern, system, method, or indicator works in all market conditions. The best you can hope for is to find a tool that will place the odds in your favor. If your winning percentage is favorable, and if your average wins are bigger than your average losses, you'll make money. The good news is that excellent technical tools are available that, when used properly, can put the odds in your favor.

An old-timer once told me, "If you can correctly identify the trend, you *will* make money." How profound. And this makes sense because if you can correctly identify the trend, the market will likely move your way. Even if your timing is initially off, the trend will often bail you out. One set of technical tools has validity for trend determination, and I have personally found them most valuable: *moving averages*. In fact, let's call the moving average "the most enough to catch one (this is over thousands of trades)—one in soybeans and one in copper. I'm not talking about a daily high or low, or even a weekly high or low, but a *major*—yearly or even quarterly—top or bottom. I'm talking about the *contract* high or low on the historical charts. Catching one of these is a very lucky and almost impossible thing to do because, in hundreds of trading days every year, there's only one major top and only one major bottom. For that matter, even minor tops and bottoms (daily or weekly highs and lows) are hard to catch because they're the exception, not the rule. During any period, every market has its top and its bottom price, but how many thousands of other trades took place even in a fairly short period of time?

An old trading adage goes something like this: "Bottom pickers get their hands slapped." As W. D. Gann has taught us, no matter how cheap or how expensive a market might appear, it's never too cheap to sell or too high to buy. As a result, I have found it much easier, and ultimately more profitable, to take a chunk out of the middle of a move. This is what moving averages are designed to do. Moving averages are *trend-following* tools. This means they do not anticipate the market—they *lag* it. They are designed to help us determine what the current trend is and when the trend has turned; however, they can tell us these things only after a trend is in place. By definition, this is after the move is already underway. Therefore, it's impossible to pick tops and bottoms using moving averages. Don't worry about missing the top, the bottom, or a portion of any move. Too many traders feel that if they haven't picked the top or bottom, it's too late to take a trade. This is one of the primary reasons that the majority of traders never make any money. Gold might have fallen $100 per ounce during a year's period and already made its low, but after it rallies $20 off the bottom, it doesn't look that cheap to most people anymore. This is because most people have short-term memories, and recent history is the history remembered first.

The previous $80 down was a tremendous short sale; anyone looking at a chart

Moving average methodologies have been around for more than a century. Richard Donchian is recognized as the modern "father of moving averages." Donchian was with the now-defunct Shearson in the late 1970s. He developed specific moving average trading techniques, and for more than 20 years, he successfully managed money using them. They were useful then and are just as useful now. This is because the markets still tend to move in *trends*—and, as you know already, *if we can accurately identify the trend of the market, we will make money.*

A Moving Picture

Any one price is similar to a snapshot in time: It cannot tell us what the trend is. It does tell us something, but hardly the whole story. When you take ten photographs in rapid succession, you can get a better picture of the whole story. If the story is the market, you get a better picture of the true trend by looking at the last ten prices, as opposed to looking at just one. When you put together a series of 20 blocks of ten photos each, you then have a movie that will be infinitely more informative than a photo or two. This movie is analogous to a *moving average line* that you can overlay on a price chart. By observing the direction this line is moving and the strength (or velocity) of the move, you can get a sense of which faction is stronger at the time—the bulls or the bears. *If the bulls are stronger than the bears, the moving average line will appear to move up, and the current price will trade above the MA, and vice versa.* The tough question when using TMVTT is how many prices give us the best feel for the trend. If we use too many, the old data can tend to put the true trend out of focus. If we use too few, we cannot really tell what we're looking at.

bigger losses. Be forewarned that drawdown periods will occur, and you must be adequately capitalized to ride these out. Finally, when using moving averages, it is extremely important for you to never lose your winning qualities of patience and discipline—particularly when the bad strings occur. This is the key to success.

Moving averages come in various flavors and sizes. They range from simple, to weighted, to smoothed and exponential. Traders use them alone or in combinations as crossovers—even triple crossovers. They use them in oscillators as moving average convergence and divergence and in bands. Our basic underlying assumption is that, more often than not, markets move in a trending fashion. I should mention that not everyone believes this is a true statement. A contingent of academics feel that market movements are random in nature (the "random walk theorists"), but I believe you can fairly easily prove to yourself that this "random walk" is bunk. Although markets can be random in a short period of time, look at any chart of any commodity of at least four to six months in length. You'll see the trends unfold before your eyes. When demand for a particular commodity or a financial asset is stronger than supply, prices (and, therefore, the market) will move in an uptrend. When supply is overwhelming demand at any particular point in time, the market will trend downward.

It's easy to determine trends after the fact by looking at a chart. For example it's easy to determine the trends in Chart A.1.

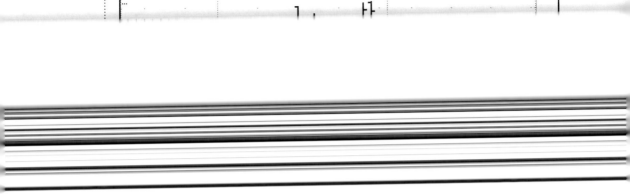

Chart A.1   December 2008 corn

However, it's not easy to determine the trends in the thick of the battle. And the news (the fundamentals) will not help you because the news is most bullish at the top and most bearish at the bottom. Plus, although markets will trend up or down, they can also move sideways. An erratic up or down period, a trendless market, temporarily wreaks havoc with any trend-following system. You'll need to use your discipline and patience to persevere in these periods. The good news is that I have found that markets are in uptrends or downtrends more often, and for longer periods of time, than they are in sideways trends. This is why moving average methodologies can put the odds in your favor.

The Simple Moving Average

The simplest moving average is simple to construct—it's called (surprise) the simple moving average (SMA). The trader can select any number of days or periods. The SMA formula follows:

SMA = (P1 + P2 + P3 + ... + PN) / N

P is the price of the commodity being averaged.

N is the number of days (or periods) in the moving average.

Let's construct a 5-day SMA of crude oil based on the closing prices. Assume that the closes during the past five days were 2105, 2110, 2115, 2120, and 2125. The 5-day SMA is 2115. If the market closes at 2155 on the sixth day, it will cause the 5-day SMA to rise to 2125, the average of the last five days divided by 5.

$$5SMAday1 = (2105 + 2110 + 2115 + 2120 + 2125) / 5 = 2115$$

$$5SMAday2 = (2110 + 2115 + 2120 + 2125 + 2155) / 5 = 2125$$

In the formula, you always drop the oldest closing price and add the most recent closing price. In this example, when using the 5-day SMA, you always drop the sixth-oldest day. With a 10-day SMA, you drop the eleventh-oldest day, and so on. The trend direction is determined by the direction the SMA is moving and by comparing today's settlement price with the moving average. In this simple example, the trend is up because the close on the most recent day—we'll call this day 2 (2155)—is higher than the SMA (2125). On day 1 (the previous day), the close was 2125 and the SMA was 2115, so the trend is up. Even with this limited data, the odds suggest that we should play from the long side. On day 2, the close was 2155 and the SMA 2125, so the trend is up and we stay long. *When the closing price turns down and under the average, a sell signal is generated.*

You can connect each day's SMA value on a chart, and this produces a line. You can chart this line and overlay it onto a price chart to generate trading signals. As long as the line on any particular day is *under* the closing price, the trader would stay long because the SMA has determined that the trend is up. After the line *crosses over* the closing price, the trader would go short because the trend has turned down. If long and the line crosses over the closing price, the trader would reverse the position by selling double the number of contracts owned. The problem is that if you do this every time the li

the price at the close could be far above or below the MA. For example, if you waited for the close on Black Monday 1987 (the day the Dow closed 500 points lower than Black Friday), you were in deep water. This is why good money-management sense says to always additionally use an ultimate "down-and-out point" for any position—a physical stop loss. You should do this when using any technical system (or fundamental, for that matter). When using an MA technique, place your stop to create an approximate maximum percentage loss for those abnormal moves. Abnormal moves, although quite rare, do occur and your first rule is to *always* avoid the catastrophic loss—the one so big that it renders us unable to continue trading. Incidentally, option strategies can also help here. You can use puts to protect long positions and calls to protect short positions. However, most markets are normal. And in normal markets, a general rule of thumb for our first simple yet effective trading system is this: On the close, if the market price has fallen *below* the moving average line, a sell signal is generated. On the close, if the market price has *risen* above the moving average line, a buy signal is generated.

You can take the signal at either the close of the signal day or the open of the following day. The preferred method is the close of the signal day because it has been proven that when a market closes at an extreme of a day's price range (which often creates the signal), it will follow through in the direction of the close the following day. Sometimes the violation of the MA could be a close call. On those days, I would opt to wait one more day instead of risking taking a false signal. However, you need to know on a daily basis exactly where the average you are following will be coming into the close, and use a "stop close only" order to enter a new position or exit an existing one. Alternatively, you can place a market order just before the close.

change the major trend, is enough to push the MA in the opposite direction of the settlement price, resulting in a false position change. It is false simply because the trader will subsequently need to reverse once again when the major trend reasserts itself. It's important to use an MA that is long enough so that it is not overly sensitive. However, if the MA is too long, the trader will tend to take too big a loss (or give up too big a portion of unrealized paper profits) before even being aware of a trend change. A longer MA will keep you in a trade longer, thereby maximizing paper profits, but it can eat into realized profits because it moves too slowly. Similar to the story of the three bears, the MA cannot be too hot or too cold; it needs to be "just right." The most popular question I'm asked centers on what is the "right" moving average to use. We discuss the "right" moving average to use (in my opinion) in greater length, but the bottom line is this: "Just right" is not always that easy to determine and will change with market conditions. Voluminous studies have been done to determine which length is right for which specific market, but I believe that these are useless because market conditions change for all markets. The silver market of the Hunt era is not the same silver market of today. Soybeans in a drought market act far differently than in a normal weather market.

Disadvantages of the SMA

The majority of traders who use moving averages use SMAs because they are simple. They are easy to calculate, but I don't always recommend them because the oldest price has the same influence as the newest. Generally, the newest price reflects current market conditions better than the oldest; however, the SMA weights them equally. For example, suppose wheat is trading between 490 and

510, and the simple 9-day SMA is about 500. However, the price was 475 on
one day of data. When this low number becomes ten days old, this lower price

composed of 200 snapshots, the last 20 will most likely tell you more about
what's probably coming next than the first 20. This is where exponential and
weighted moving averages come in. They place more weight on the newest
prices, and this can be more valid than the older prices when determining the
true trend.

Exponential and Weighted Moving Averages (EMA and WMA)

The exponential and weighted moving averages assign a greater weight to more
recent events. The WMA increases the importance of the most recent price by a
factor equal to the period used. For example, with a 5-day weighted average, the
fifth day is given a factor five times greater than the first. To calculate a 5-day
weighted average, multiply day 5 (the most current day) by 5, day 4 by 4, day 3
by 3, day 2 by 2, and the first, or oldest, day by 1 and then divide by 15. The
EMA also weights recent events more than distant events, but it smoothes out
the average for a more consistent result. The smoothing factor (SF) is determined by dividing 2 into the moving average plus 1 of the SMA you want to
weight and smooth. For example, if you want to smooth a 5-day SMA, you
divide 2 by 6. The result, .33, is the smoothing factor. For a 10-day SMA, the
SF is 2 ÷ 11 = .18. For a 20-day SMA, the SF is 2 ÷ 21 = .096. The SF is a
fixed weight applied to the current price, with the balance applied to the most
recent moving average value itself. Let's look at a specific example to make this
clearer. Let's calculate a 5-day SMA and a 5-day EMA for wheat. Remember, we
need at least 5 days of data to produce our starting point for the SMA. Suppose
the closing (settlement) prices for 11 consecutive days of wheat prices are as
follows:

Day	Price
10	476
11	481

We can easily see *in hindsight* from this data that the trend was up during this 11-day period (the market gained 41¢). However, hindsight is always 20/20, and it's not always easy to know just what the trend actually is when we're in the thick of the battle. This is where moving averages can help.

The SMA is calculated as follows:

Day	Price	Calculation	SMA
1	440		
2	446		
3	461		
4	446		
5	463	(440 + 446 + 461 + 446 + 463) / 5	451.2
6	458	(446 + 461 + 446 + 463 + 458) / 5	454.8
7	472	(461 + 446 + 463 + 458 + 472) / 5	460
8	470	(446 + 463 + 458 + 472 + 470) / 5	461.8
9	464	(463 + 458 + 472 + 470 + 464) / 5	465.4
10	476	(458 + 472 + 470 + 464 + 476) / 5	468
11	481	(472 + 470 + 464 + 476 + 481) / 5	472.6

If you used the 5-day SMA to generate buy or sell signals, starting on day 5, you would have been a buyer at the closing price of 463 (because the price was

factor, which is .67, times the EMA.

Day	Price	Calculation	EMA
1	440	Start	440
2	446	$[(.33 \times 446) + (.67 \times 440)]$	441.98
3	461	$[(.33 \times 461) + (.67 \times 441.98)]$	448.26
4	449	$[(.33 \times 449) + (.67 \times 448.26)]$	448.5
5	463	$[(.33 \times 463) + (.67 \times 448.5)]$	453.29
6	458	$[(.33 \times 458) + (.67 \times 453.29)]$	454.84
7	472	$[(.33 \times 472) + (.67 \times 454.84)]$	460.5
8	470	$[(.33 \times 470) + (.67 \times 460.5)]$	463.64
9	464	$[(.33 \times 464) + (.67 \times 463.64)]$	463.76
10	476	$[(.33 \times 476) + (.67 \times 463.76)]$	467.8
11	481	$[(.33 \times 481) + (.67 \times 467.8)]$	472.15

The results show that the price remained above the EMA during the entire period, even day 9. *Therefore, no whipsaw resulted.* The trader would remain long from 446 and still be long on day 11 at 481. Yes, you can still get whipsawed using the EMA in a choppy market, but in general, I've found that WMAs and EMAs are superior moving averages, with fewer whipsaws.

Many traders are using moving average systems with a percentage band (such as the Bollinger bands) that uses an exponentially smoothed moving average plus a band above this EMA and minus a band below the EMA by the same

Summary

Moving averages are not the Holy Grail and are not all created equal; however, if used systematically and consistently, they tend to keep a trader on the right side of the big moves. They are a totally technical approach (they rely on price only), and it doesn't matter which market you use them on. They work well in bull and bear markets and in both the stock and commodity markets; however, they'll whipsaw the trader in a sideways or trendless market. However, this isn't as big of a disadvantage as it might appear at first, because my experience has shown that markets will spend more time in trending modes than trendless modes. But periods with choppy, whipsaw-type markets have lasted for many weeks. Sometimes a seasoned trader can sense that a market is trendless (the time to step to the sidelines) but not always. And if not properly capitalized or disciplined during these periods, a trader can be wiped out or, at the very least, become demoralized and abandon a moving average program. Usually the trader will quit just before the big move starts. Remember that you need to catch the big moves when using a moving average system or you won't win.

Section 2: Open Interest

Open interest (OI) analysis is a powerful trading tool that futures traders use. (Stock traders do not have it.)

The Open Interest Primer

OI is simply the number of contracts outstanding, the total number held by buyers *or* (*not* and) sold short by sellers on any given day. The OI number gives you the total number of longs and the total number of shorts because, unlike in

pears from the OI statistics. If a new buyer buys from an old buyer (who is selling out), total OI remains unchanged. If a new seller buys back or *covers* from a new seller entering the market, OI also does not change. The old bear had to buy to cover, with the other side of this transaction being a sell by the new bear.

Let's look at a typical example. If heating oil has a total OI of 50,000 contracts, and the next day it rises to 50,100, this means 100 new contracts were created by 100 new buyers and 100 new sellers—or perhaps ten new net buyers and sellers of ten contracts each, or whatever it takes net to create the new 100. During that day, many people closed out and many entered, but the net result was the creation of new OI. The market has 50,100 contracts' worth of shorts and 50,100 contracts' worth of longs at the end of the day. Theoretically, one short who had 100 new contracts sold (probably the smart money) could have taken the opposing side of 100 others who each bought one (the majority, probably the dumb money), but the short and long interest are always the same on any particular day.

The exchanges release OI figures daily, but they are always for the *previous* day, so they are a day old. A trader can chart OI on a price chart, and the direction it is changing can tell you some interesting things.

The Advanced OI Course

OI statistics are a valuable tool that you can use to predict price trends and reversals. The size of the OI reflects the intensity of participants' willingness to hold positions. Whenever prices move, someone wins and someone loses—the zero sum game. This is important to remember because when you think about the ramifications of changes in OI, *you must think about it in the context of which way the market is moving at the time.* An increase in OI shows a

Six Profit Rules for Analyzing OI

1. *If prices are in an uptrend and OI is rising, this is a bullish sign.* The bulls are in charge. They are adding to positions and making the money, thus becoming more powerful. Shorts are also being stopped out, but new sellers are taking their place. As the market continues to rise, the longs get stronger and the shorts get weaker.

2. *If prices are in a downtrend and OI is rising, this is a bearish sign.* The bears are in charge in this case. They are adding to their positions, and they are the ones making the money. Weaker longs are being stopped out, but new buyers are taking their place. As the market continues to fall, the shorts get stronger and the longs get weaker. Another way to look at the first two rules is that, as long as the OI is increasing in a major trend, it will have the necessary financing to draw upon and prosper.

3. *If prices are in an uptrend and OI is falling, this is a bearish sign.* The old longs, the smart money (I call them "smart money" because they have been right to this point), are taking profits and liquidating. They are replaced by some new buyers who will not be as strong on balance, but the declining OI is an indication that the weak shorts are also bailing. They will be replaced to some extent by new shorts that are stronger than the old shorts were.

1. *If prices are in a downtrend and OI is falling, this is a bullish sign—the*

6. *If prices are in a congestion range and OI is falling, this is a bullish sign.* The reason is that the professionals, who are more likely to be short, are covering. The weak hands are throwing in the towel.

SMA (simple moving

buy signals, generating, 93-95

of thinking

doors, a technique that solves a problem, or an insight that simply helps make sense of it all.

We work with leading authors in the various arenas of business and finance to bring cutting-edge thinking and best-learning practices to a global market.

It is our goal to create world-class print publications and electronic products that give readers knowledge and understanding that can then be applied, whether studying or at work.

To find out more about our business products, you can visit us at www.ftpress.com.